This book belong to:

....

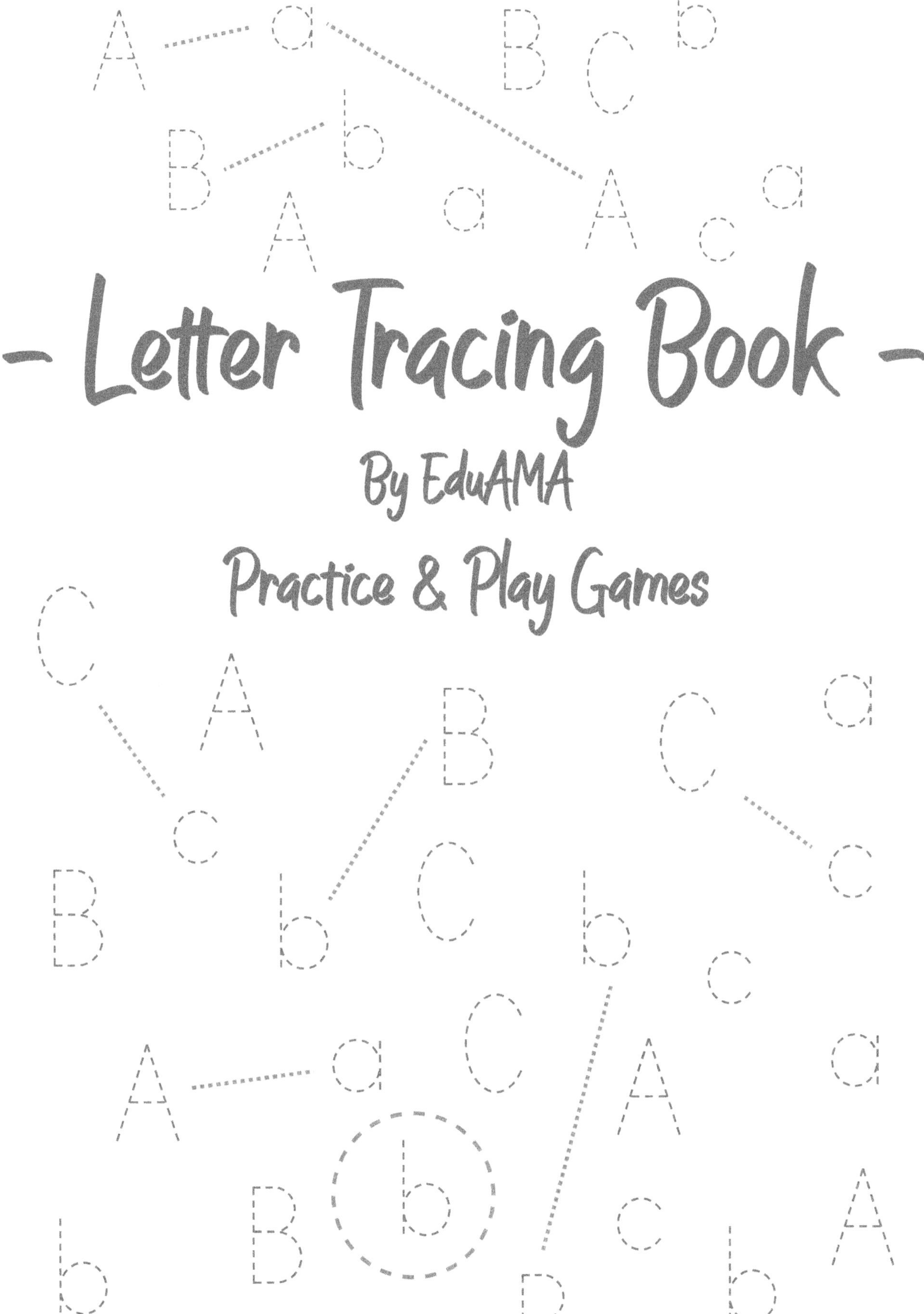

- Letter Tracing Book -

By EduAMA

Practice & Play Games

A

Apple

A A A A A A A

apple

a a a a a a

A A A A A A

A A A A A A

A A A A A A

a a a a a a

a a a a a a

a a a a a a

Banana

B B B B B B

banana

b b b b b b

B B B B B B

B B B B B B

B B B B B B

b b b b b b

b b b b b b

b b b b b b

B b

B b

C

Cake

CCCCCC

cake

cccccc

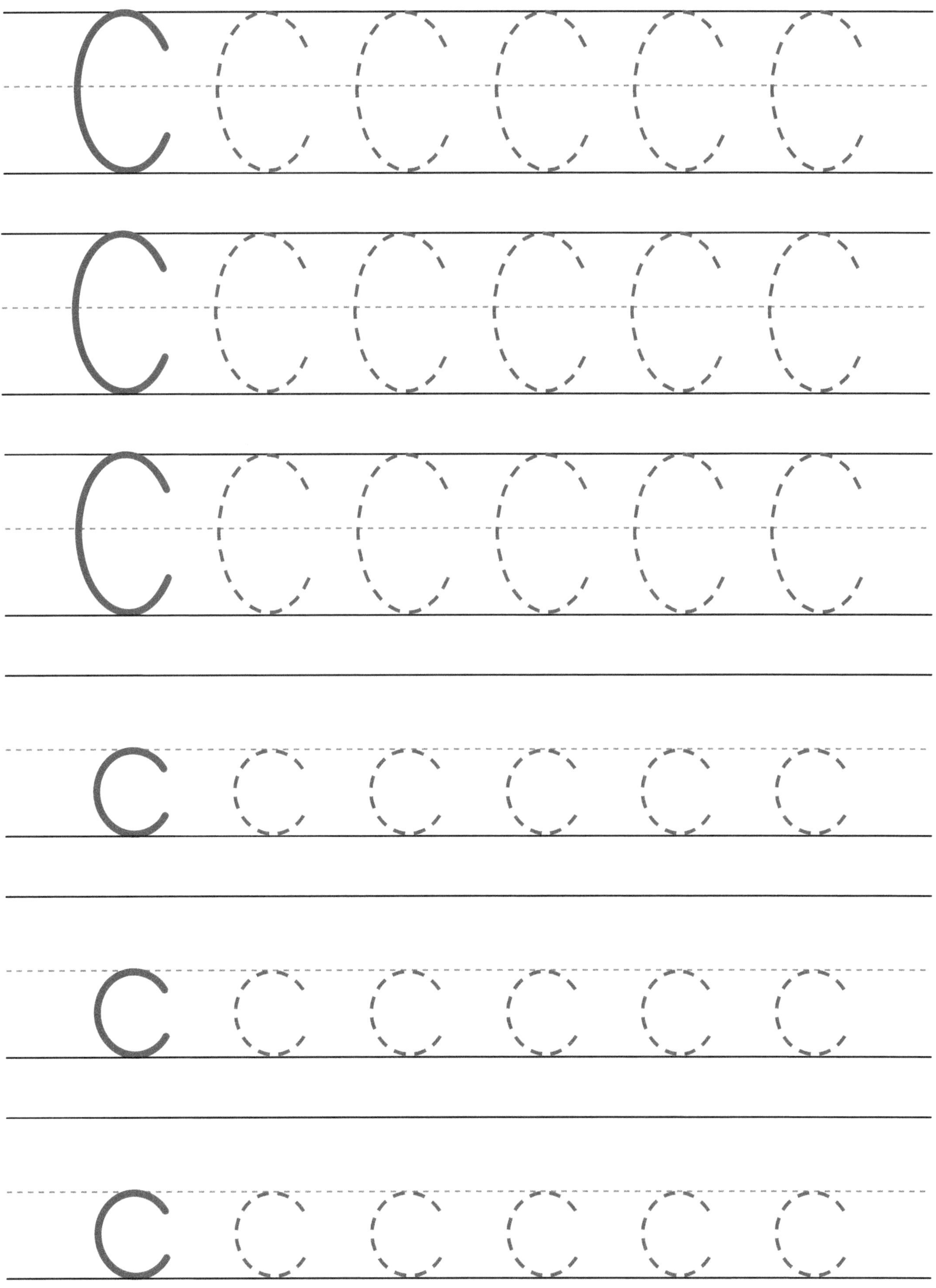

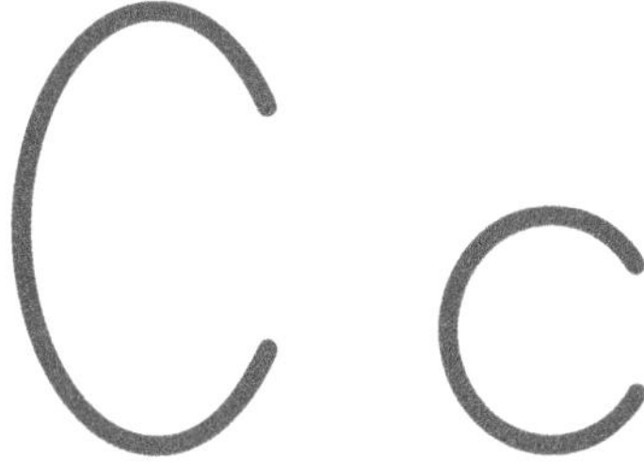

Connect

Upper case letter with its lower case

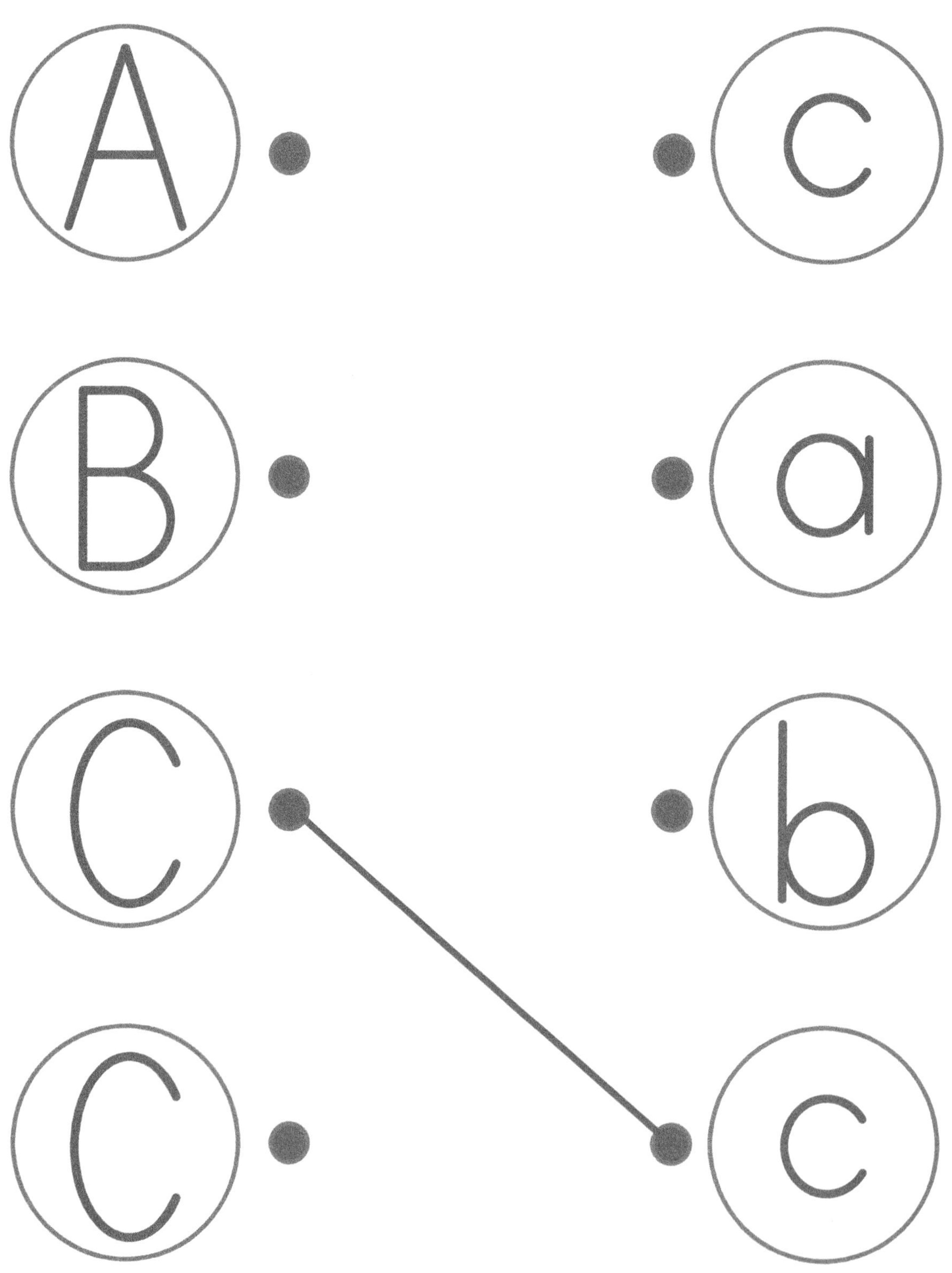

Do a circle on all letters of B
in upper case and lower case

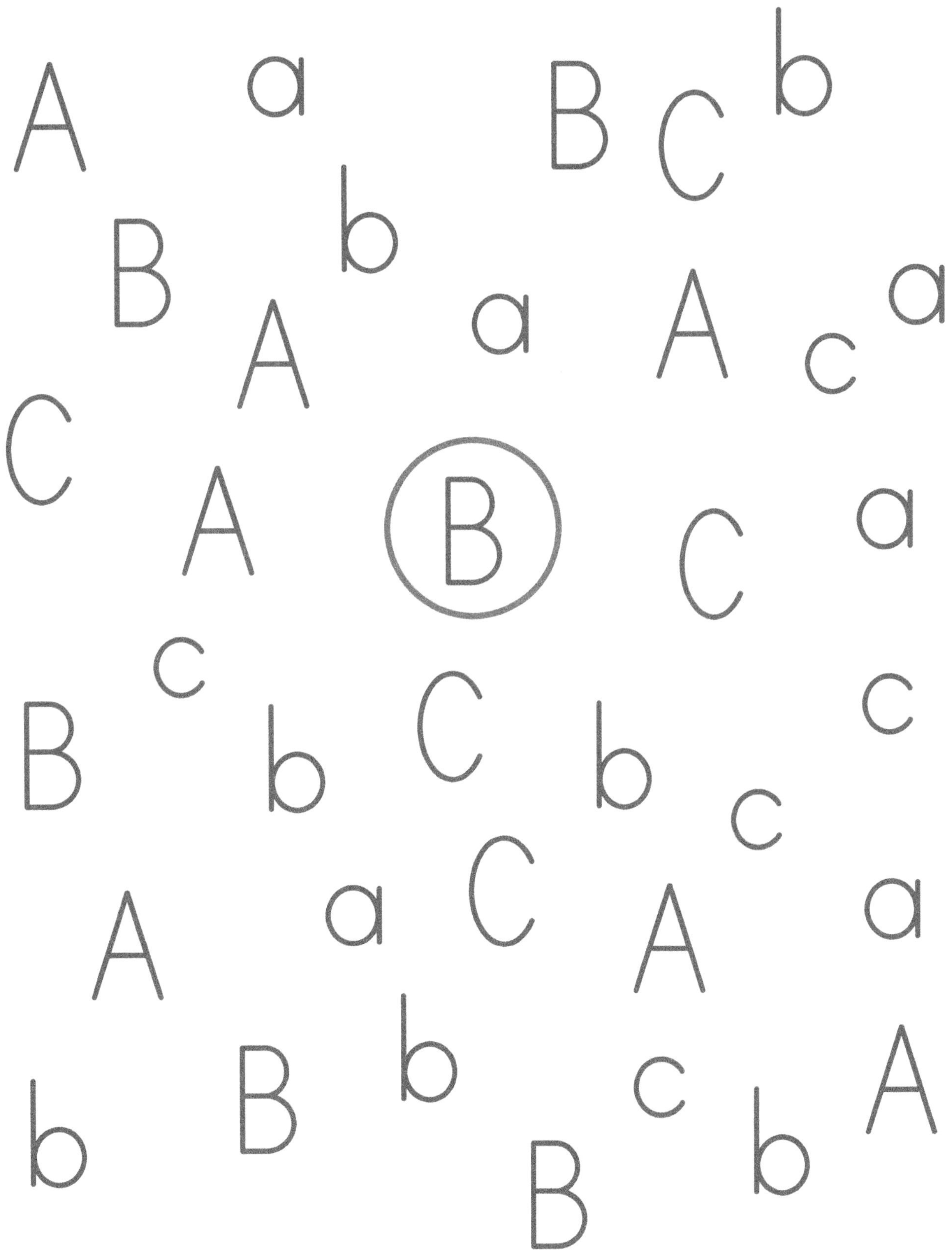

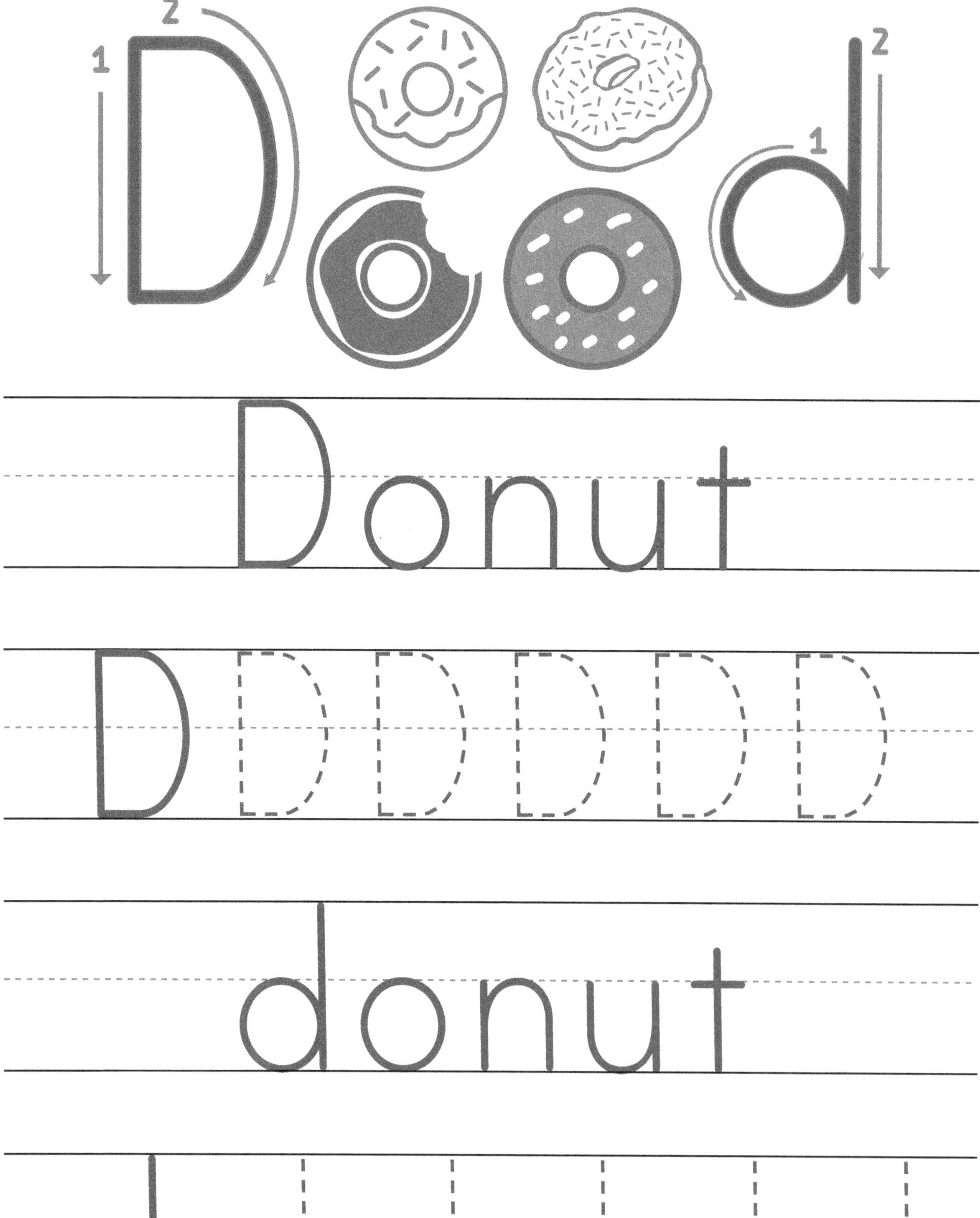

Donut

donut

D D D D D D

D D D D D D

D D D D D D

d d d d d d

d d d d d d

d d d d d d

D d

D d

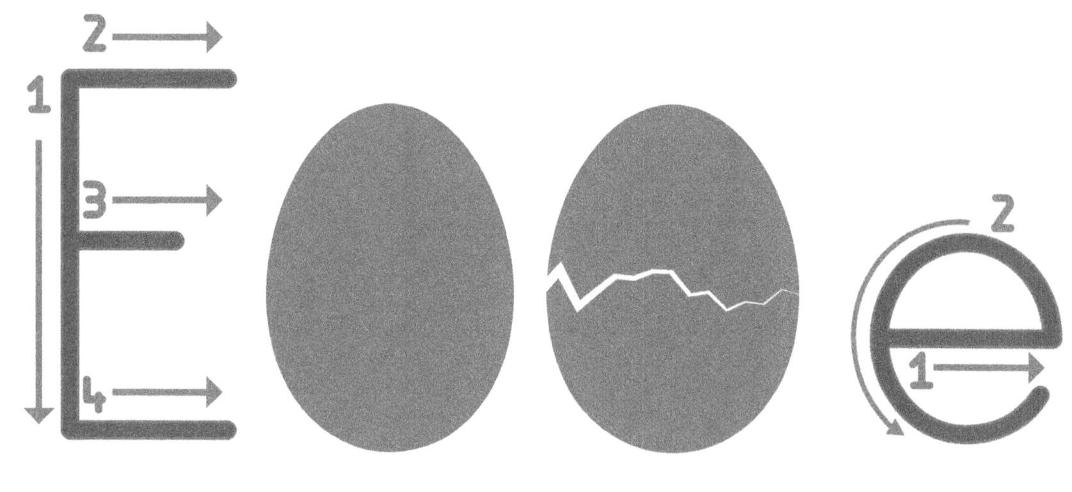

Egg

E

egg

e

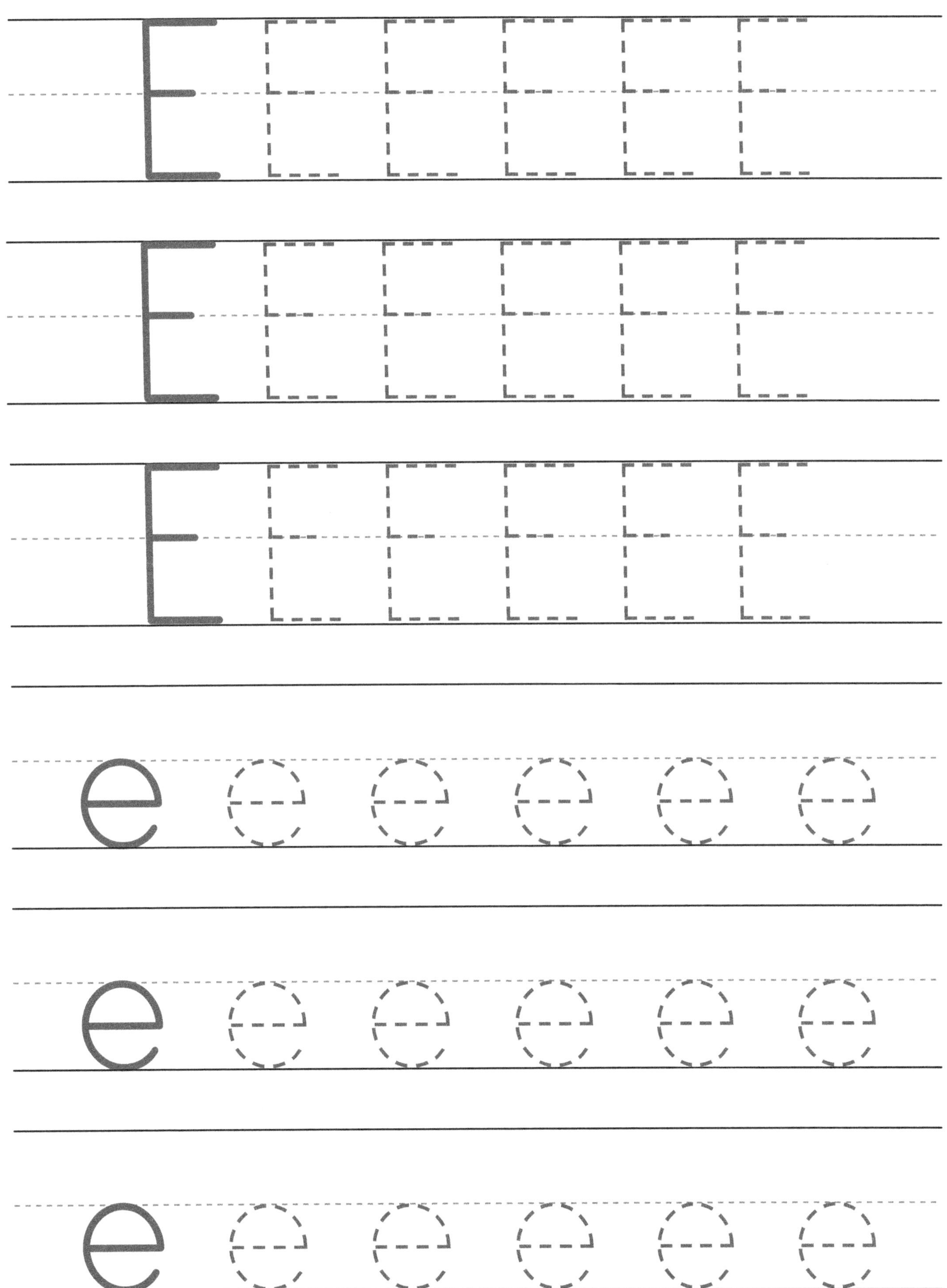

E e

Fish
F
fish
f

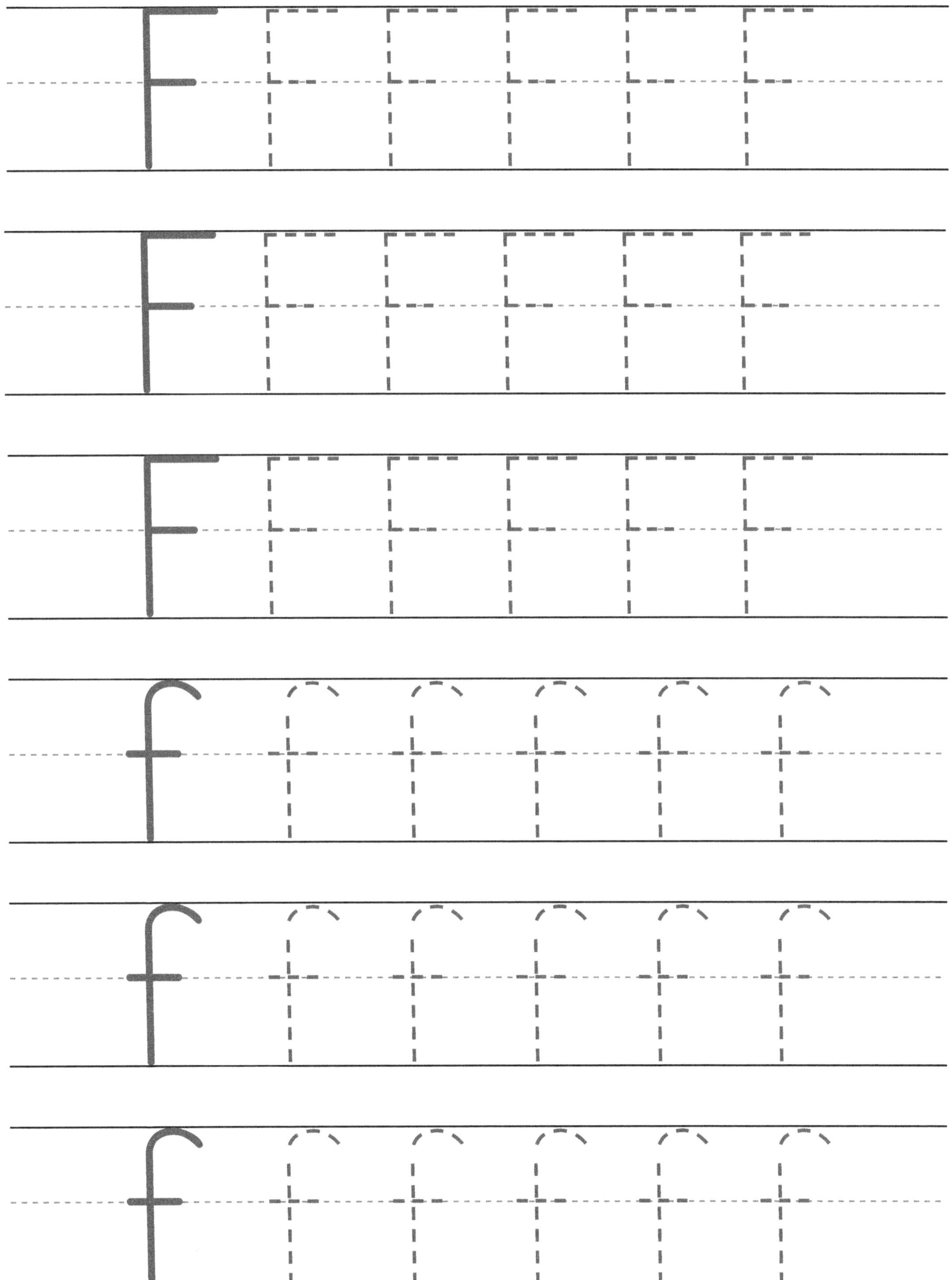

F f

F f

Connect
Upper case letter with its lower case

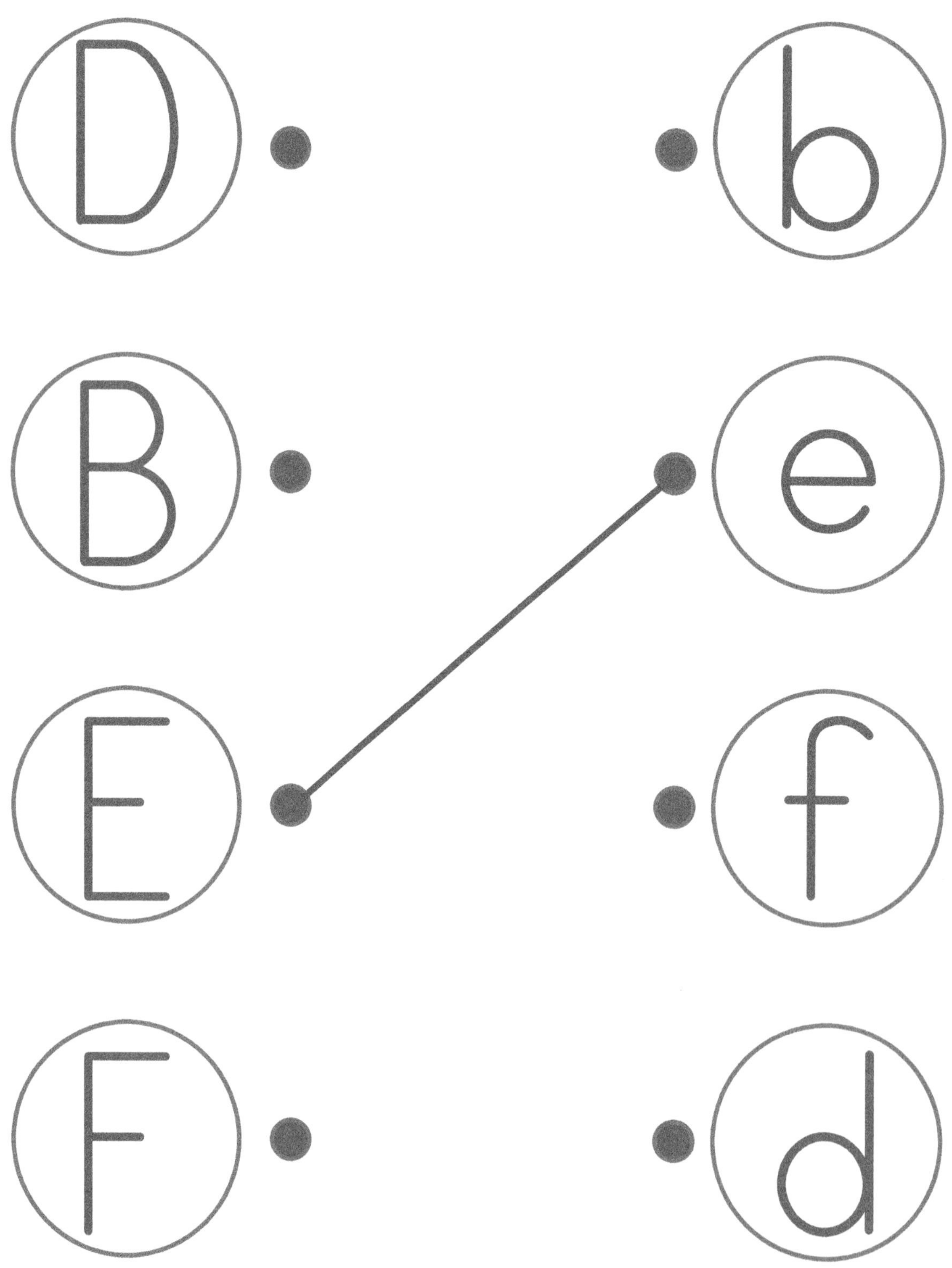

Do a circle on all letters of E
in upper case and lower case

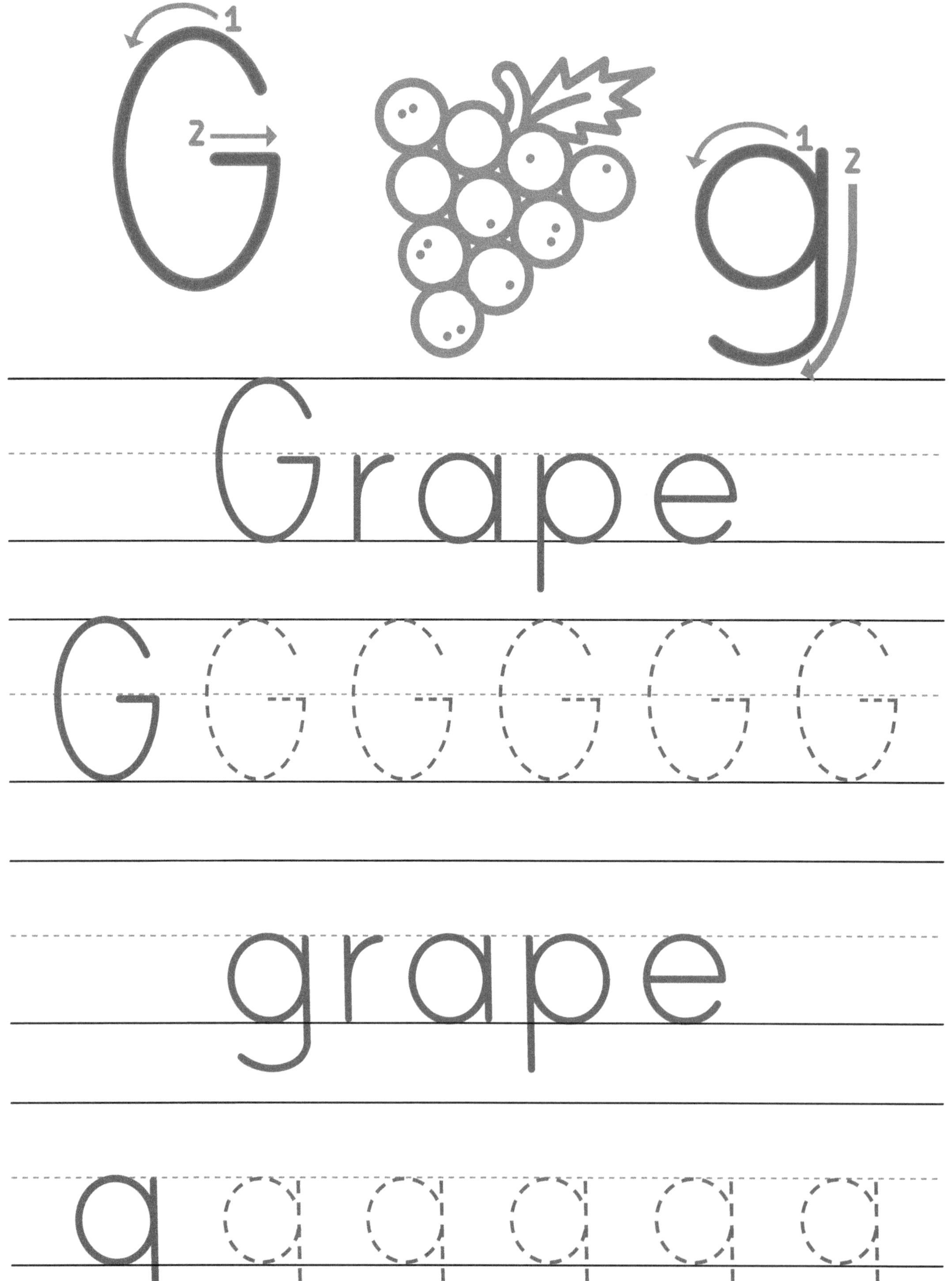

Grape

grape

G G G G G G

G G G G G G

G G G G G G

g g g g g g

g g g g g g

g g g g g g

G g

G g

1
2
3
H
1
2
h
Hat
H
hat
h

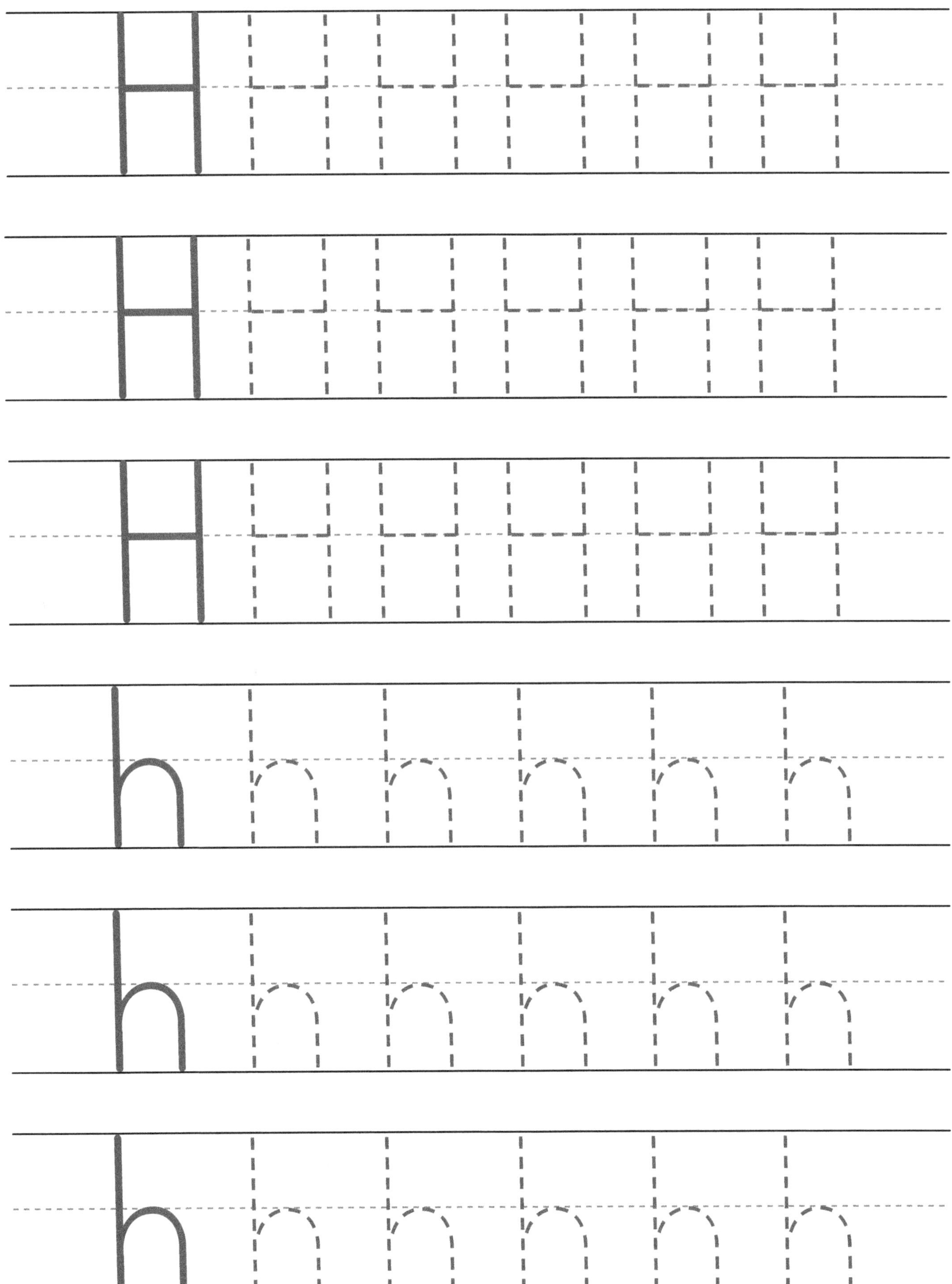

Ice Cream

I

ice cream

i

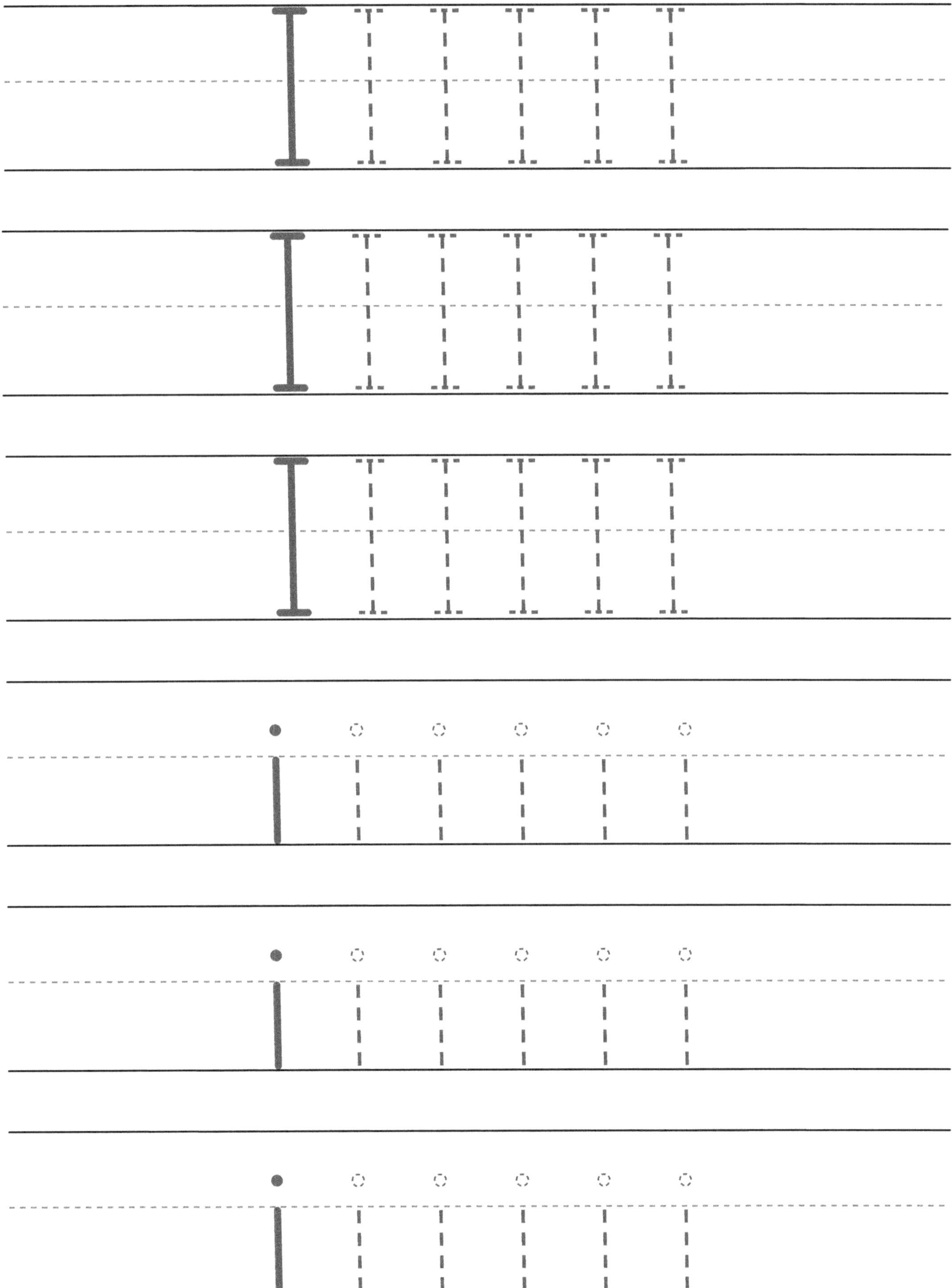

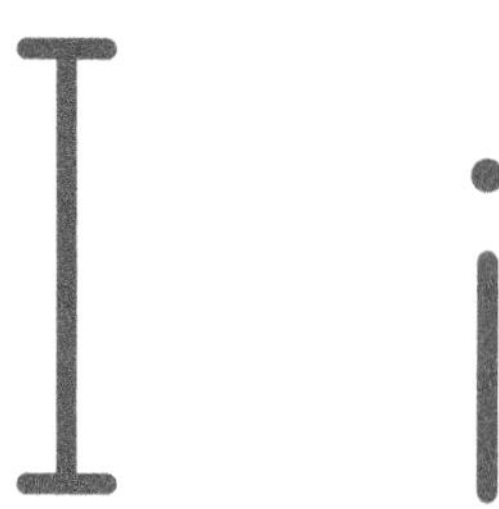

Connect
Upper case letter with its lower case

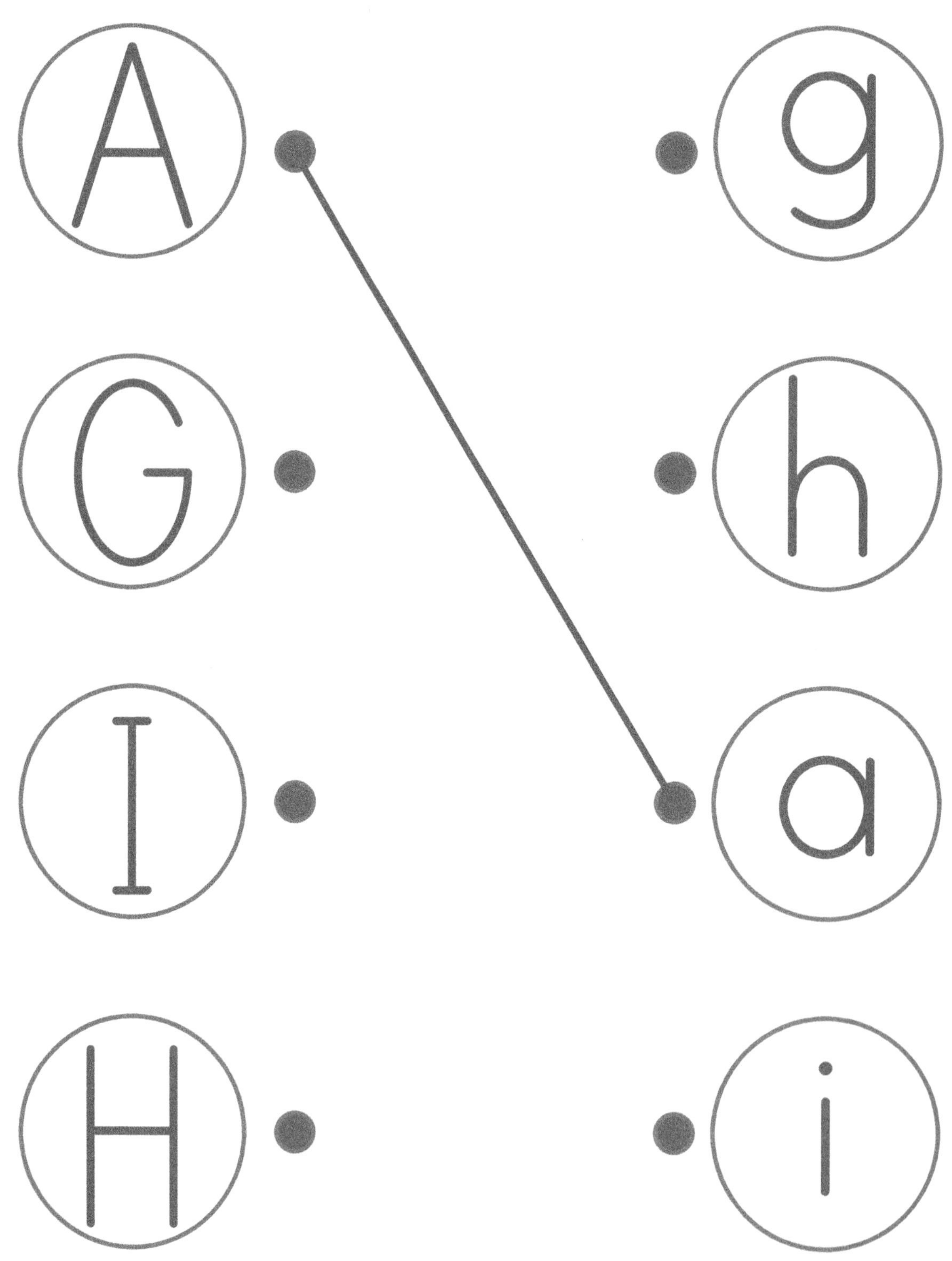

Do a circle on all letters of G
in upper case and lower case

J
j
Juice
J J J J J J J
juice
j j j j j j j

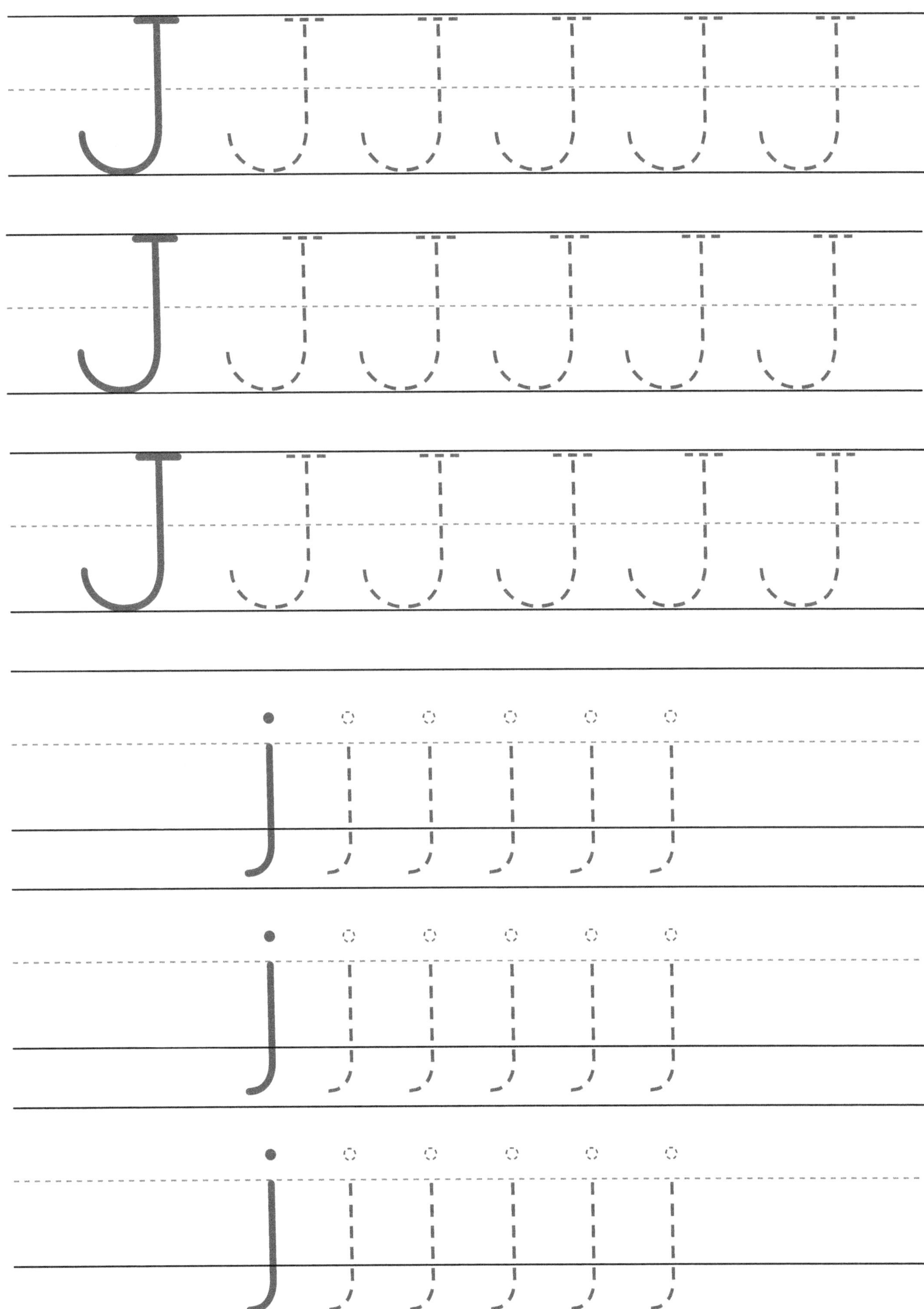

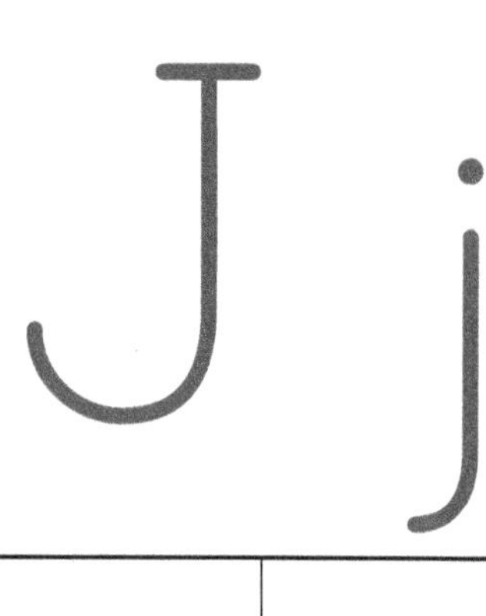

J j

Kitten

kitten

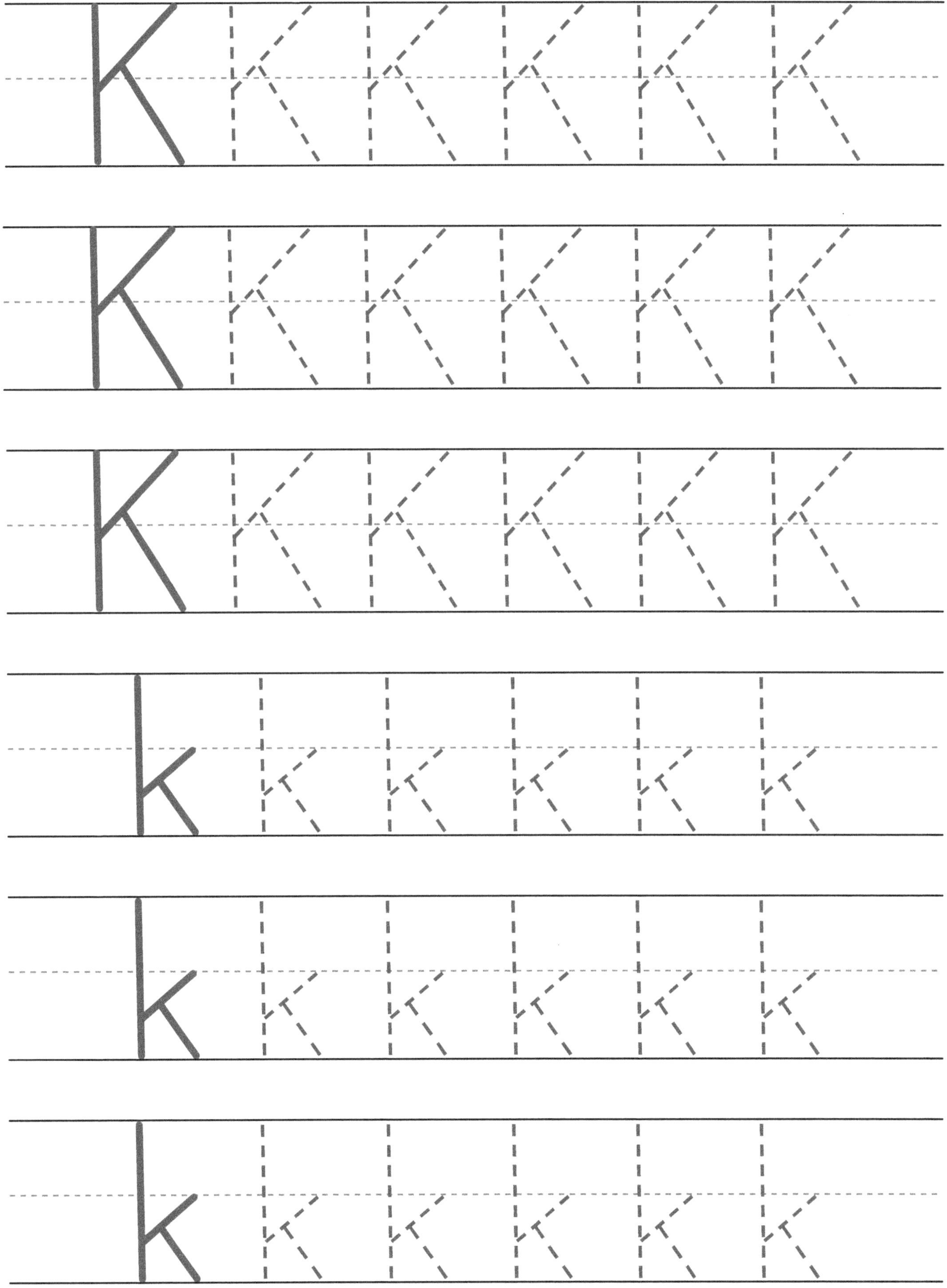

Lemon

L

lemon

l

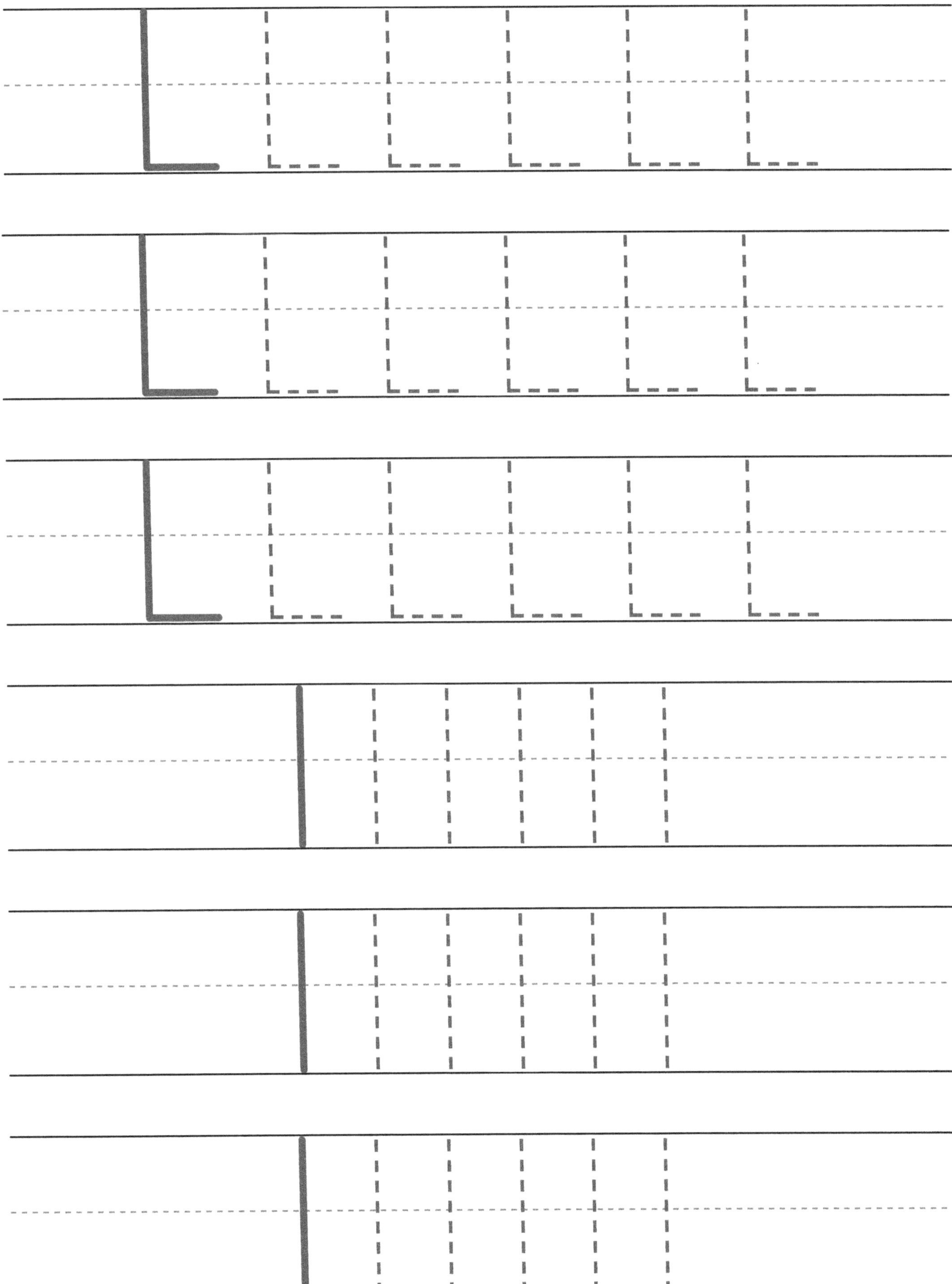

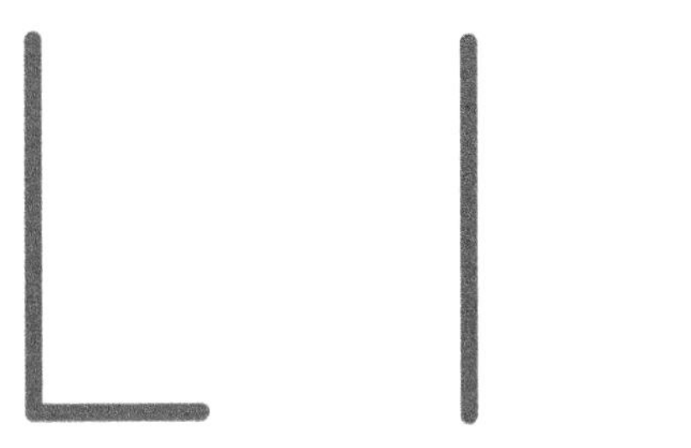

Connect
Upper case letter with its lower case

Do a circle on all letters of K
in upper case and lower case

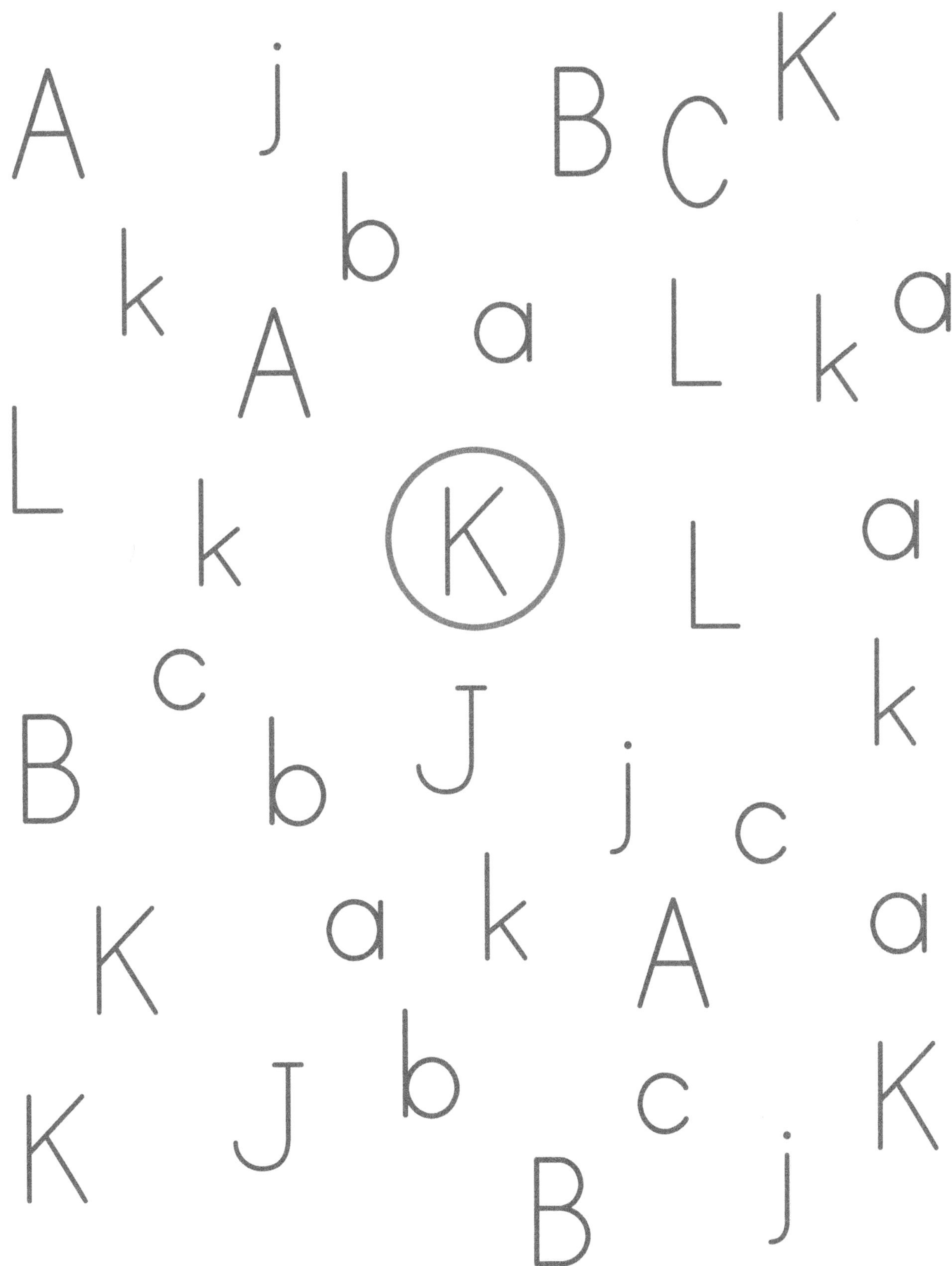

Monkey

monkey

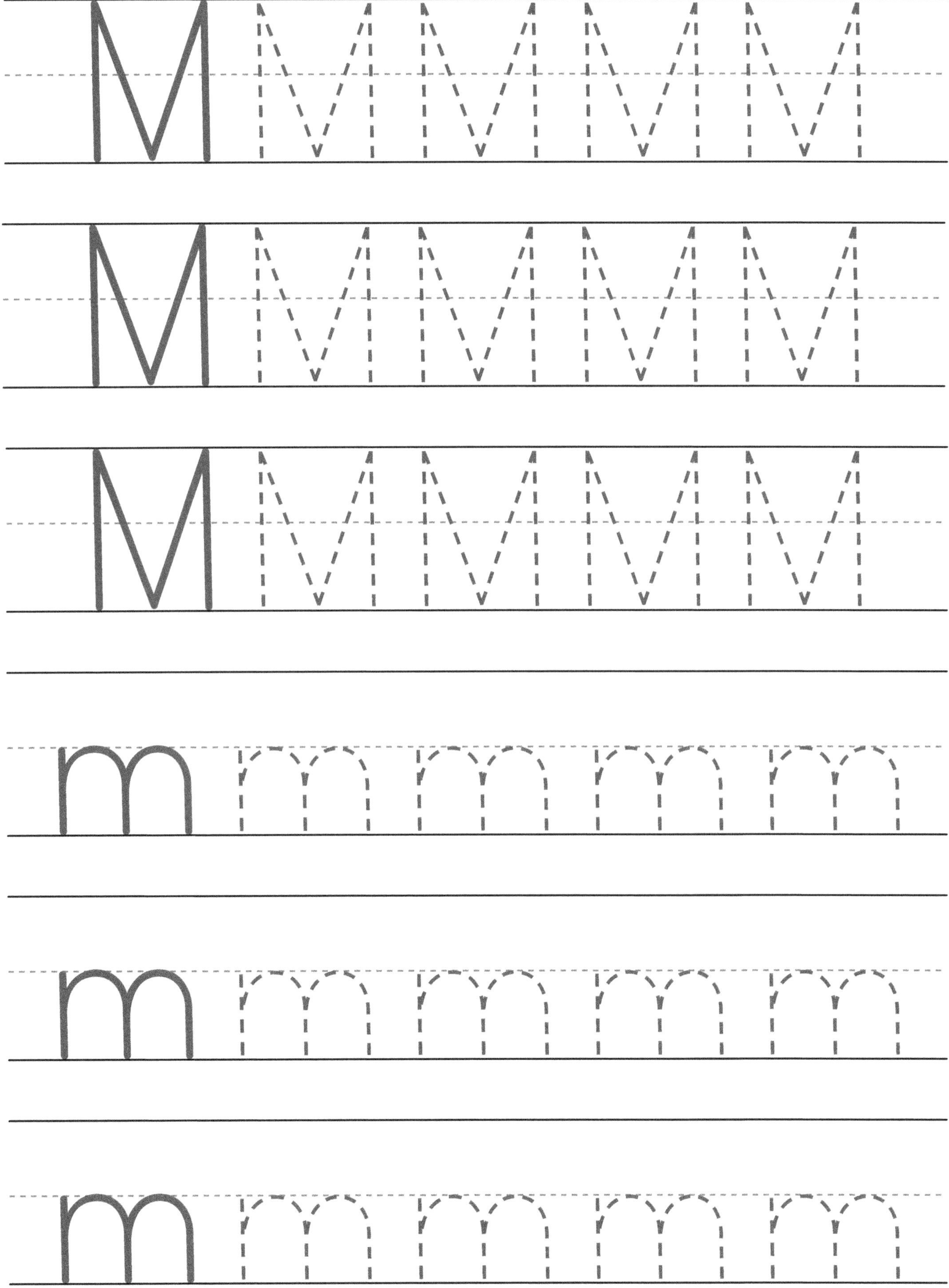

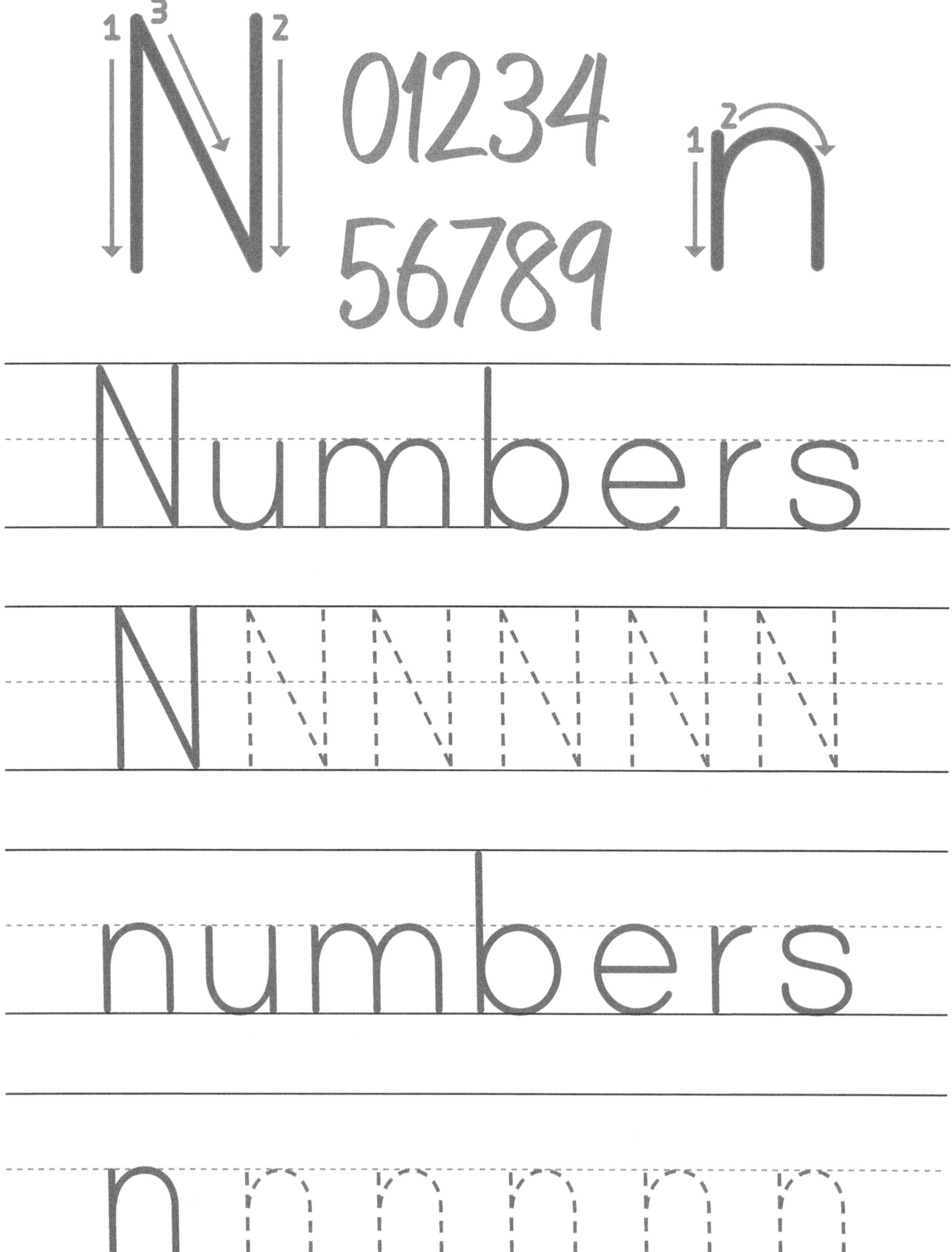

01234
56789
Numbers
N
numbers
n

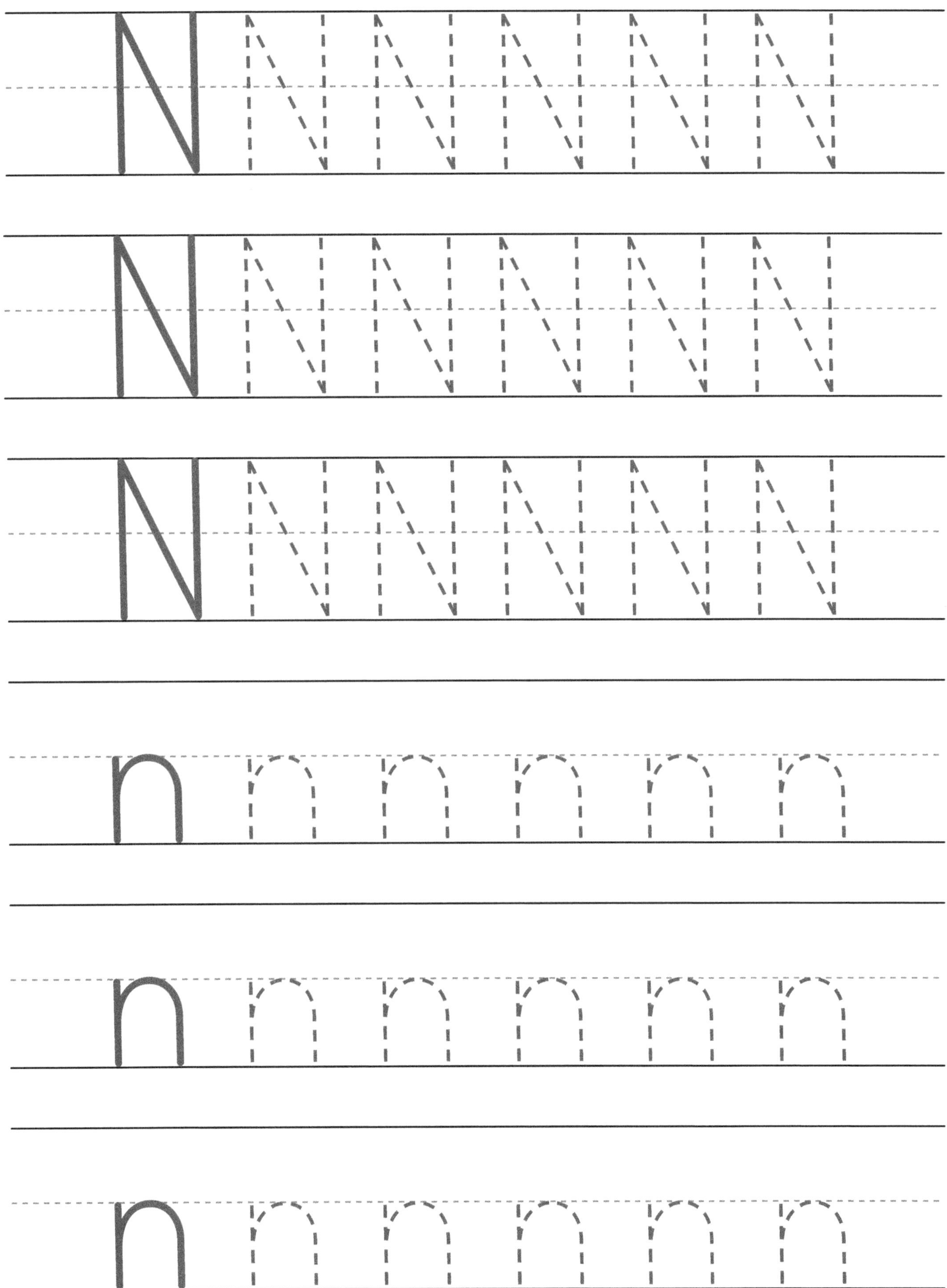

N n

Orange

O O O O O O O

orange

o o o o o o

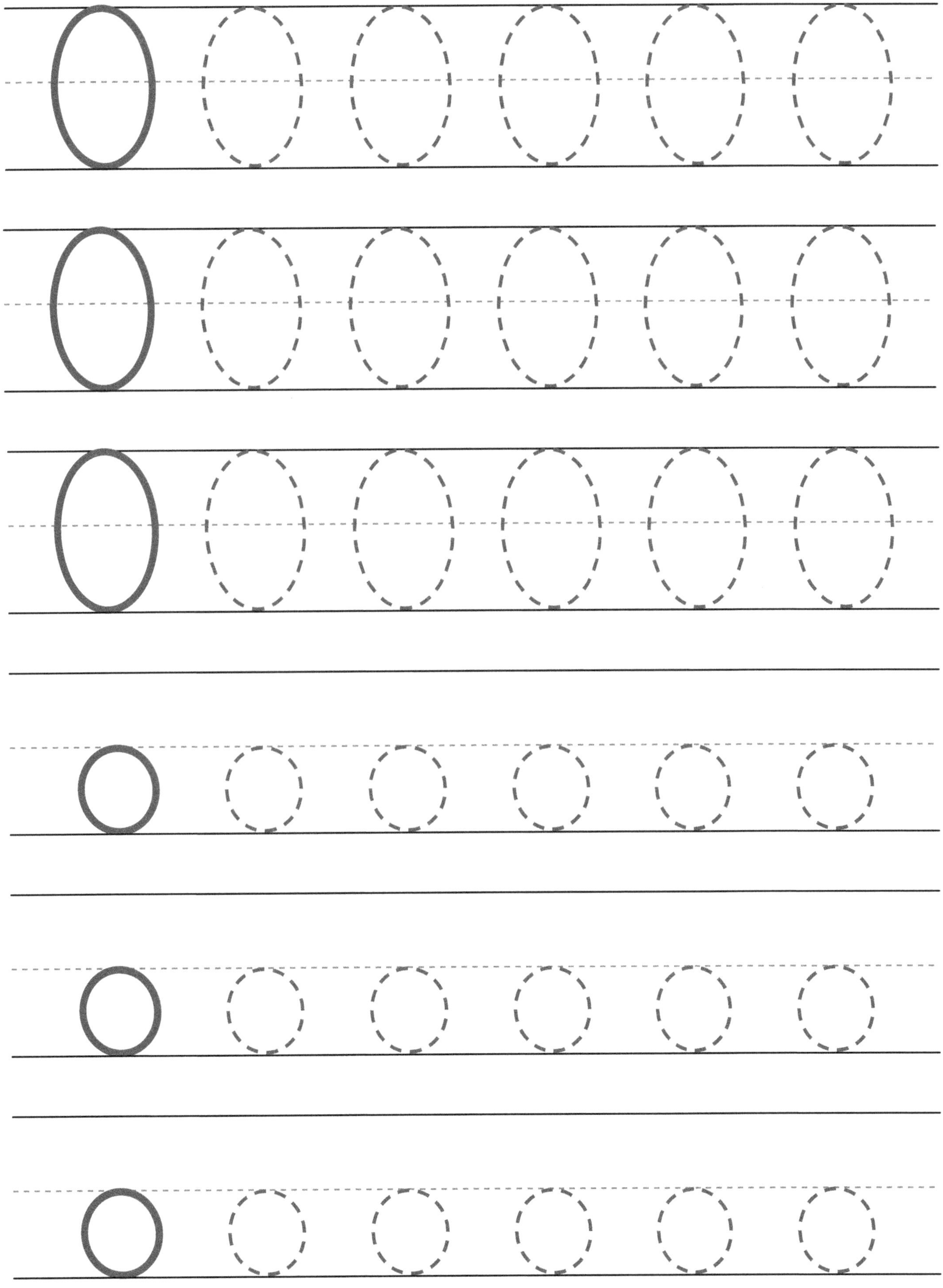

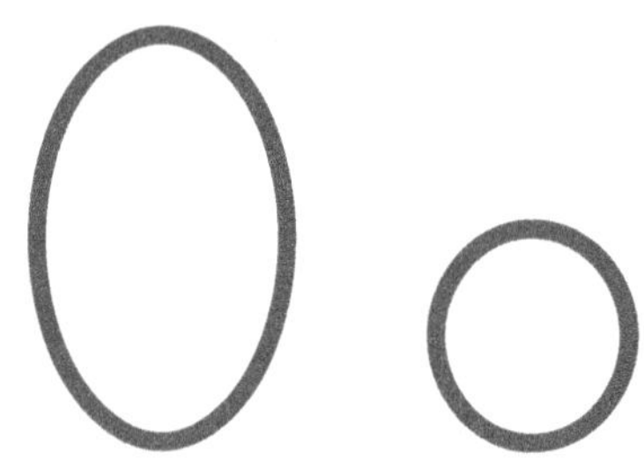

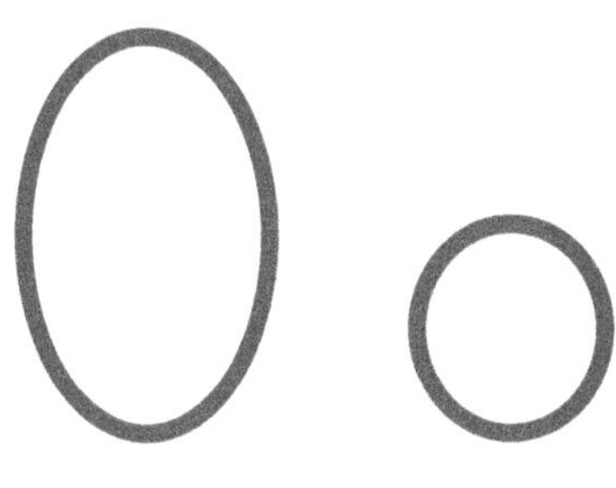

Connect
Upper case letter with its lower case

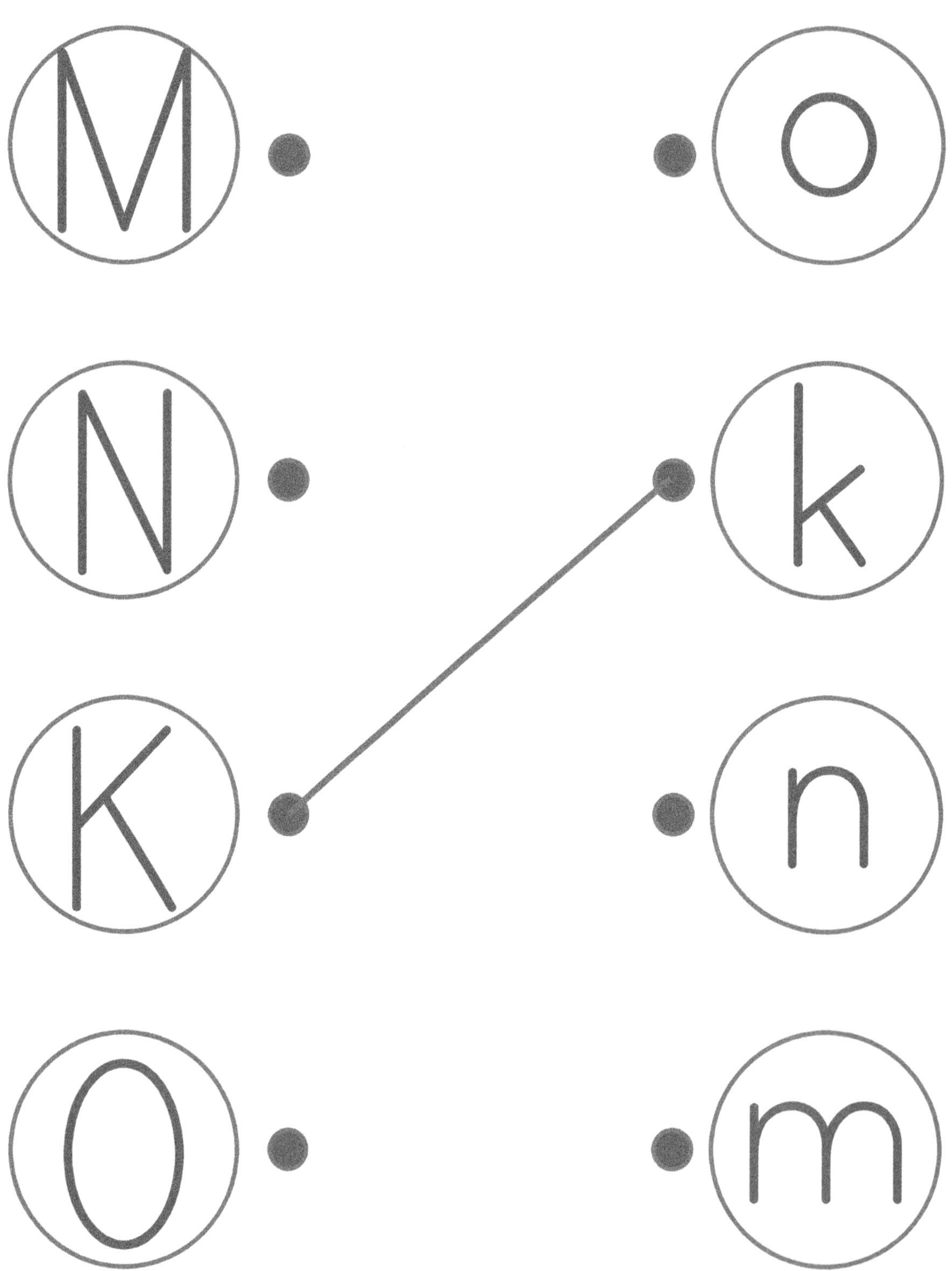

Do a circle on all letters of N
in upper case and lower case

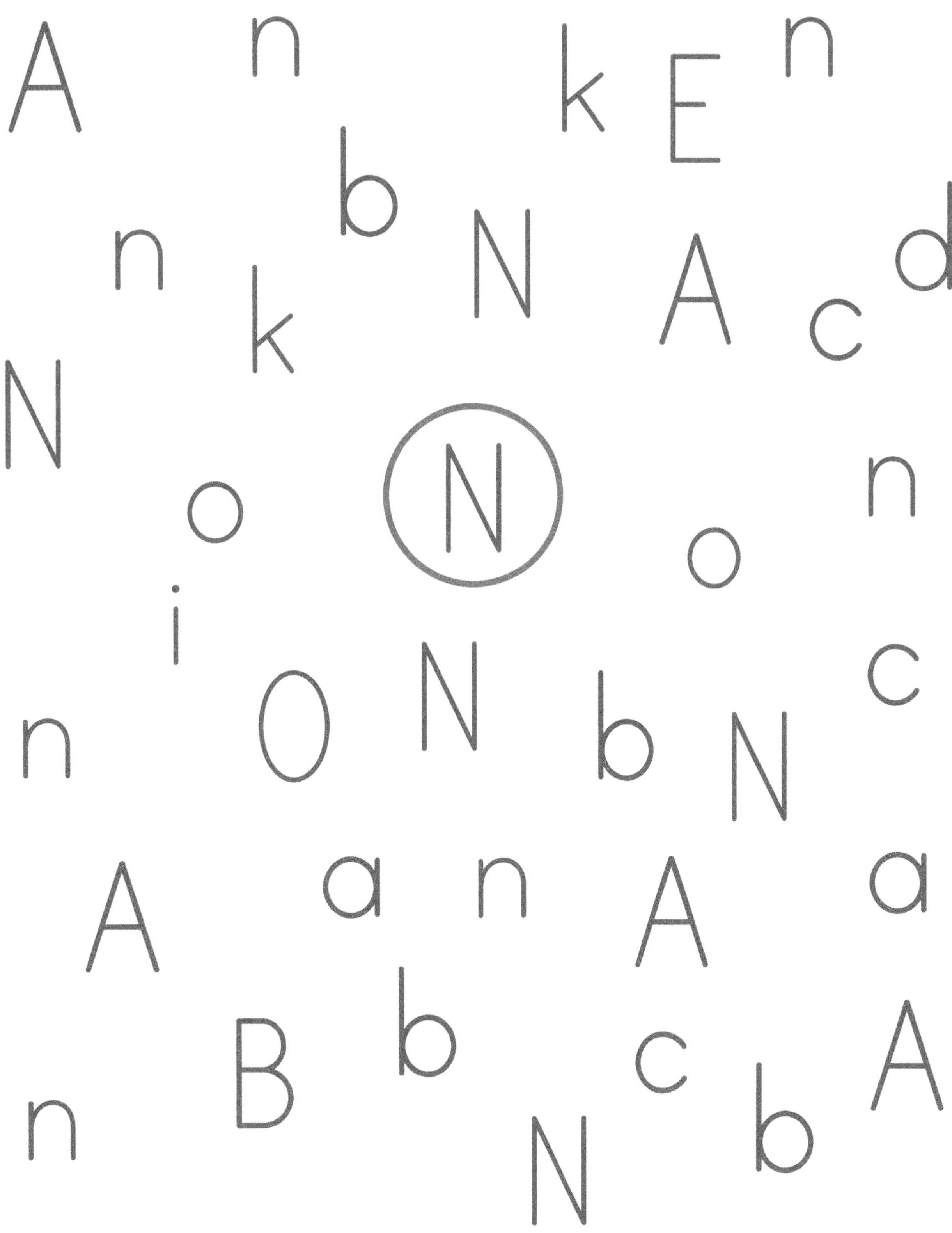

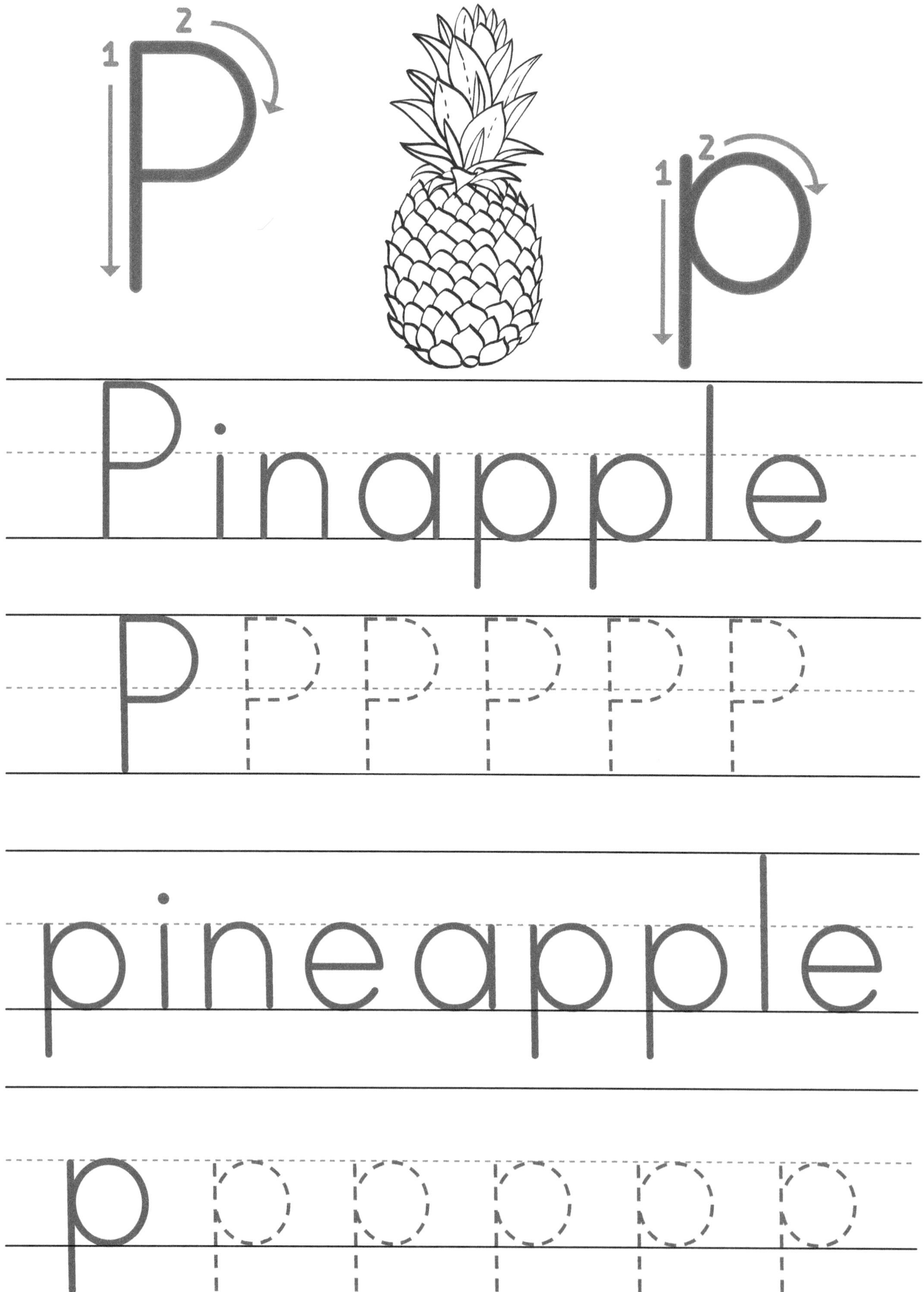

Pinapple

pineapple

P P P P P P

P P P P P P

P P P P P P

p p p p p p

p p p p p p

p p p p p p

P p

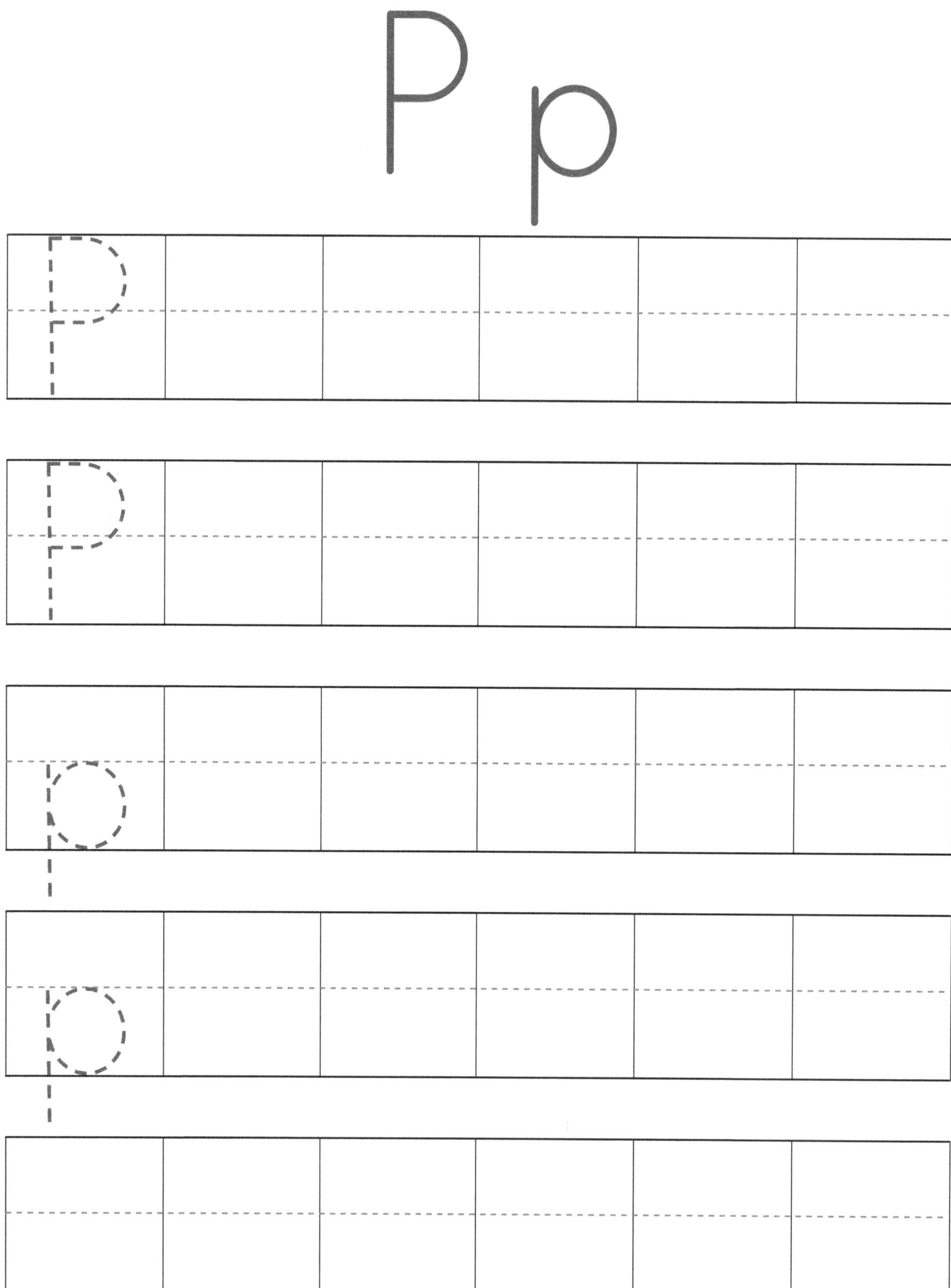

P p

1
2
1
2
Queen
Q
queen
q

Q Q Q Q Q Q Q

Q Q Q Q Q Q Q

Q Q Q Q Q Q Q

q q q q q q

q q q q q q

q q q q q q

Q q

Q q

Rabbit

R R R R R R

rabbit

r r r r r r

R R R R R R

R R R R R R

R R R R R R

r r r r r r

r r r r r r

r r r r r r

R r

Connect
Upper case letter with its lower case

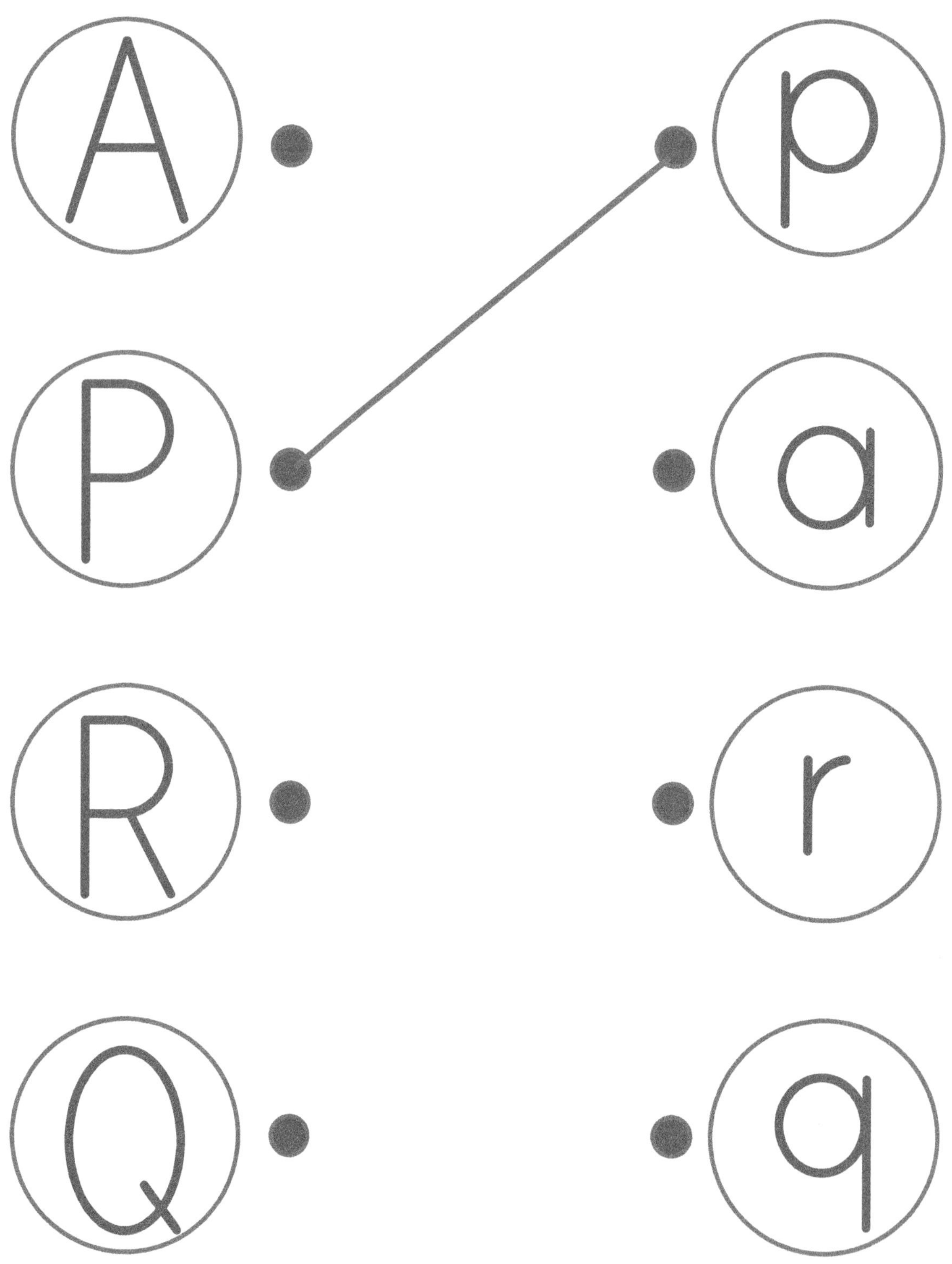

Do a circle on all letters of R
in upper case and lower case

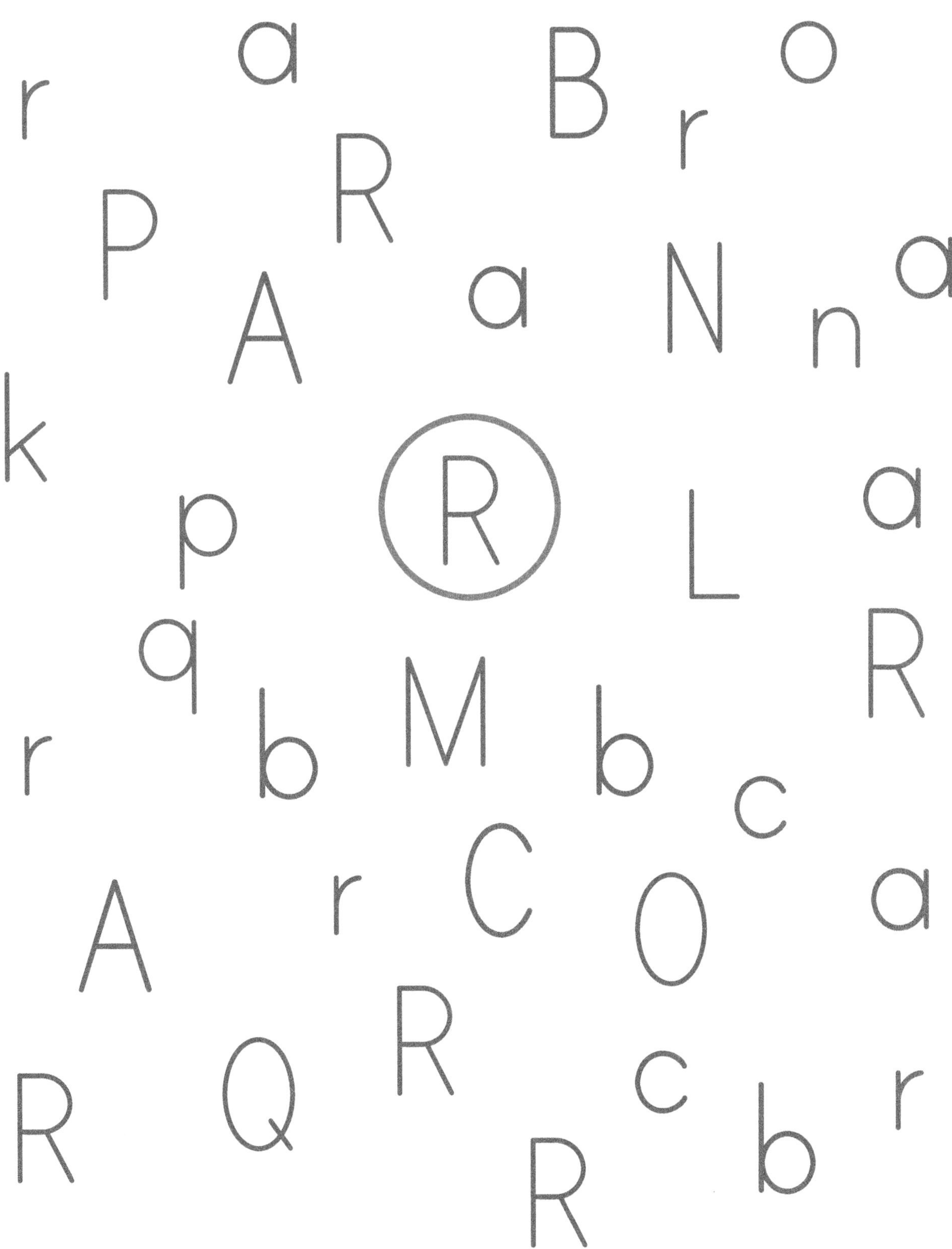

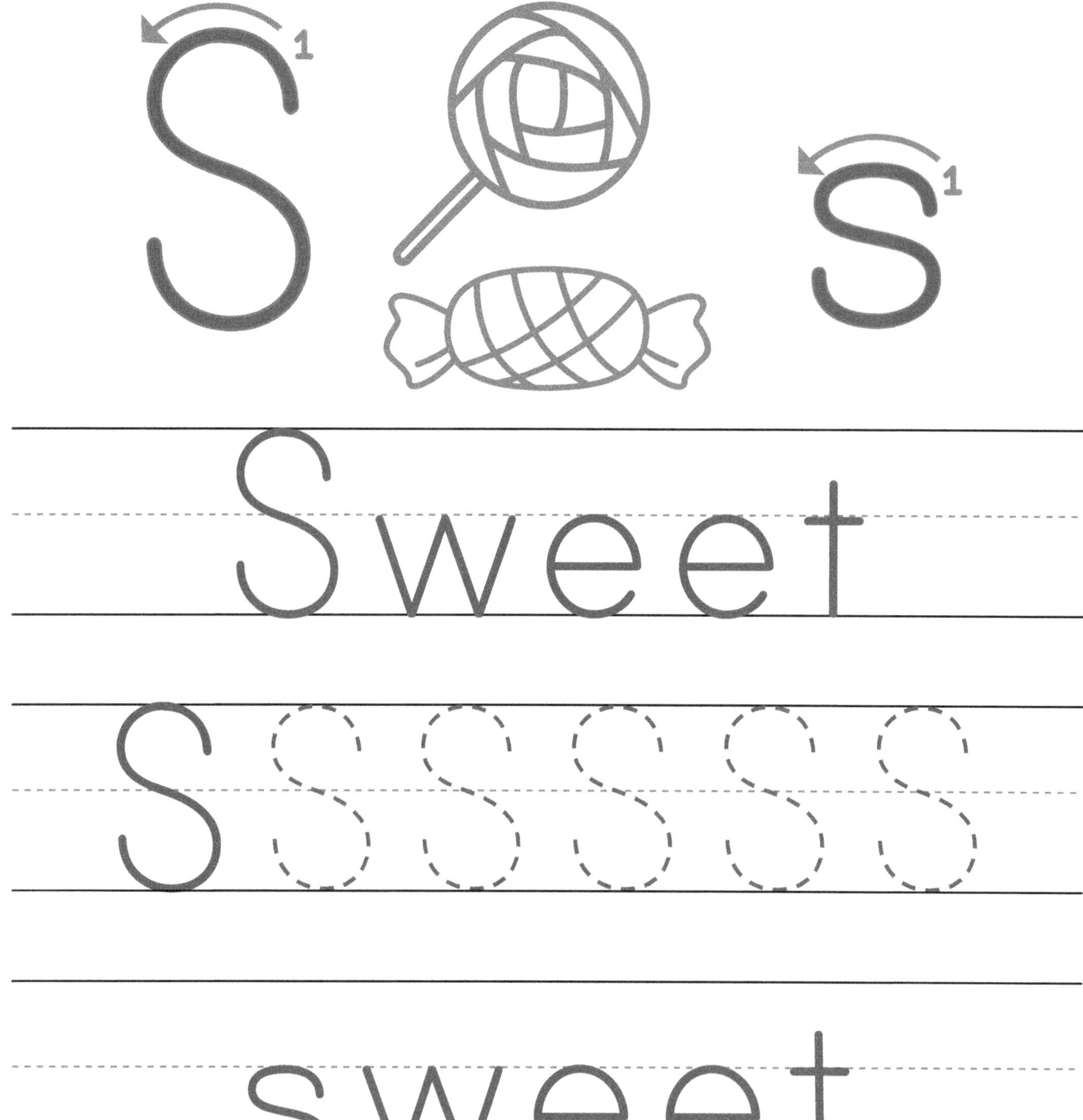

Sweet

sweet

S S S S S S
S S S S S S
S S S S S S
s s s s s s
s s s s s s
s s s s s s

S s

S s

Tomato
T
tomato

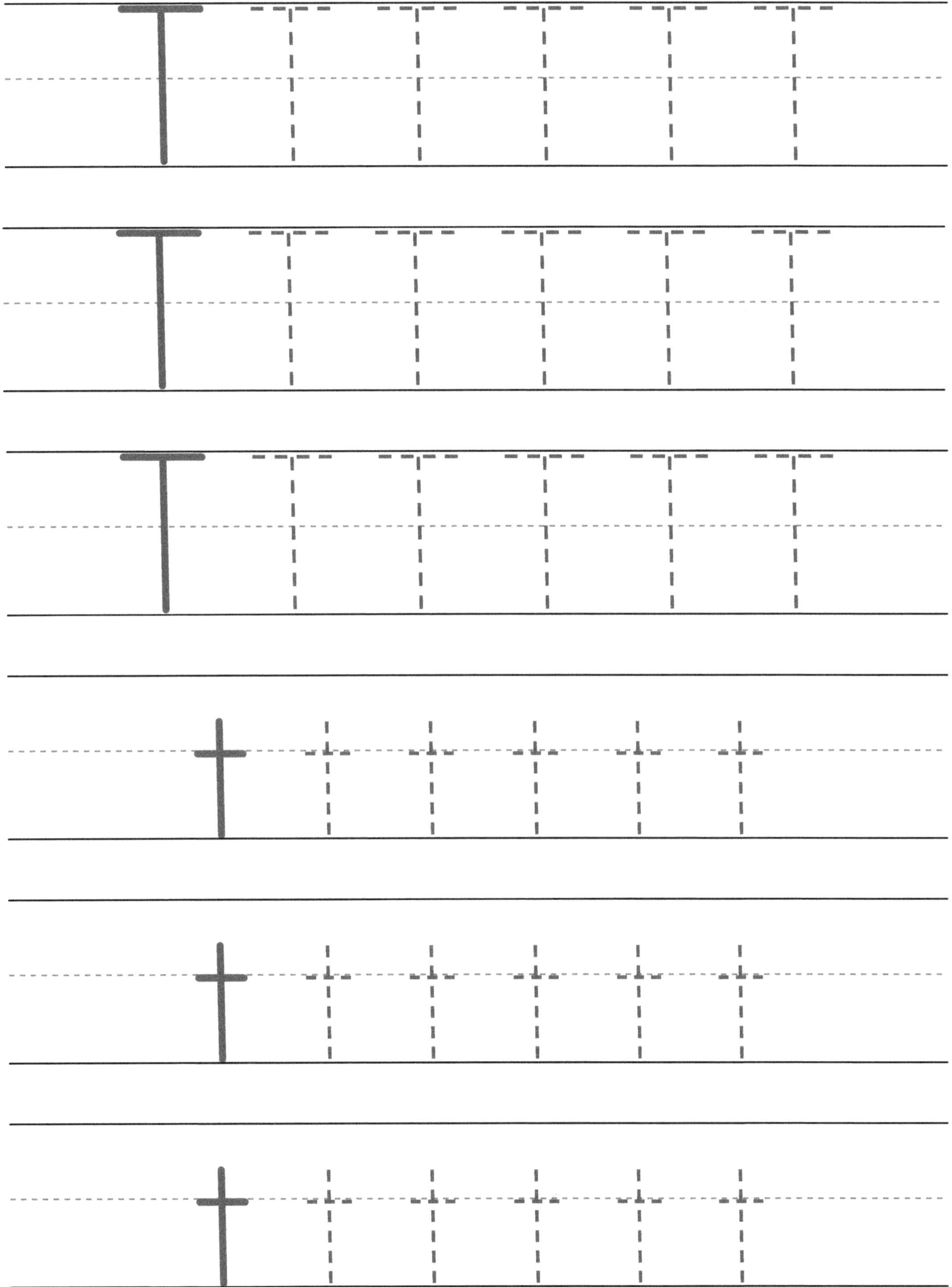

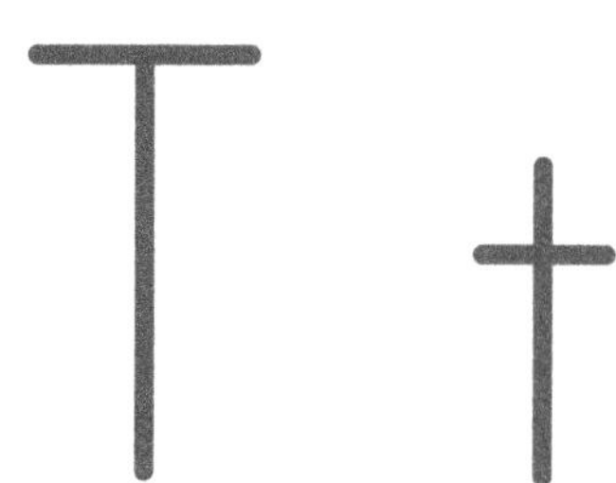

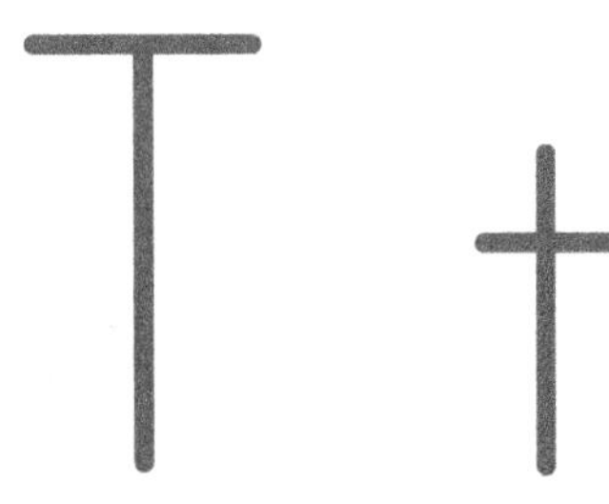

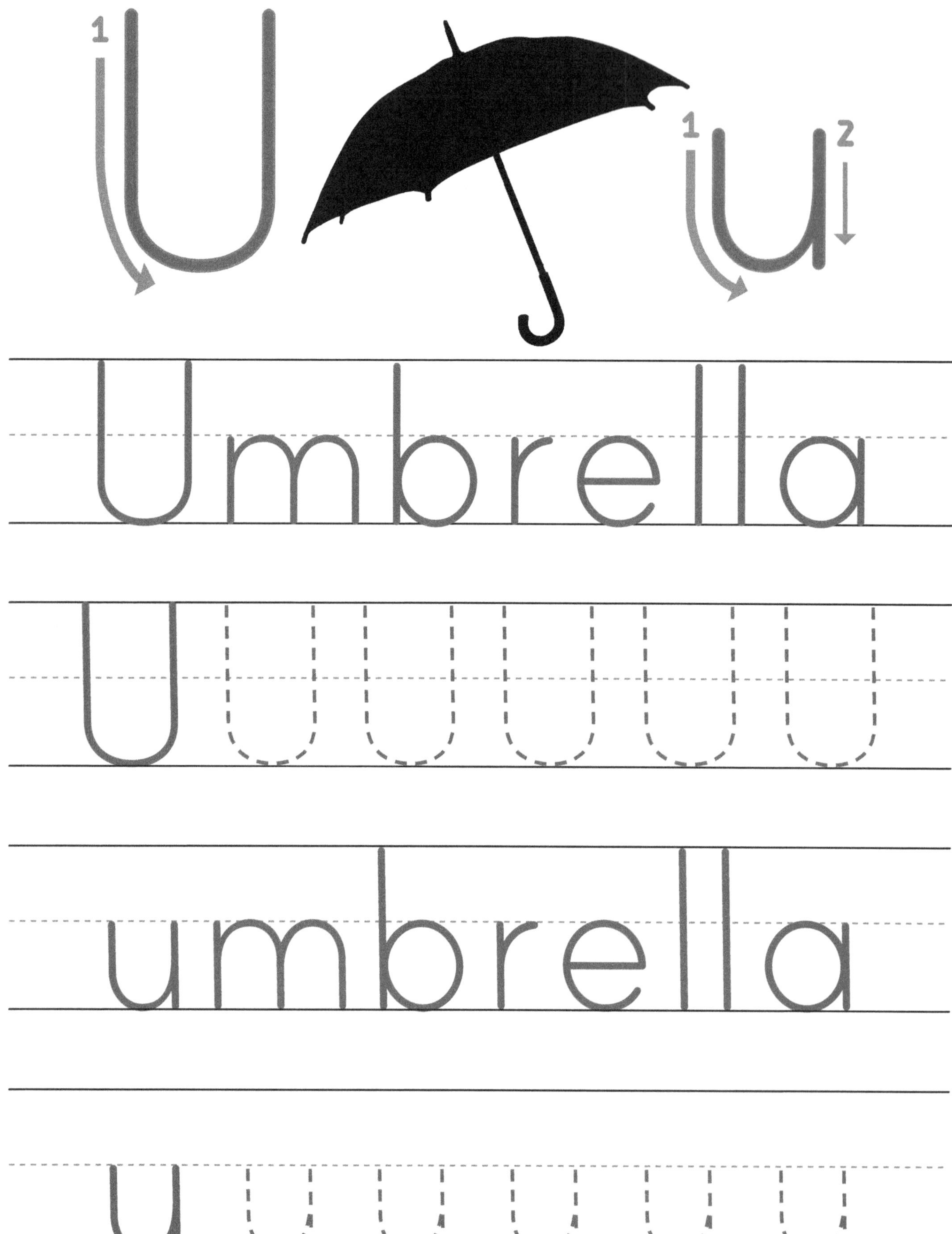

1
1 2
Umbrella
umbrella

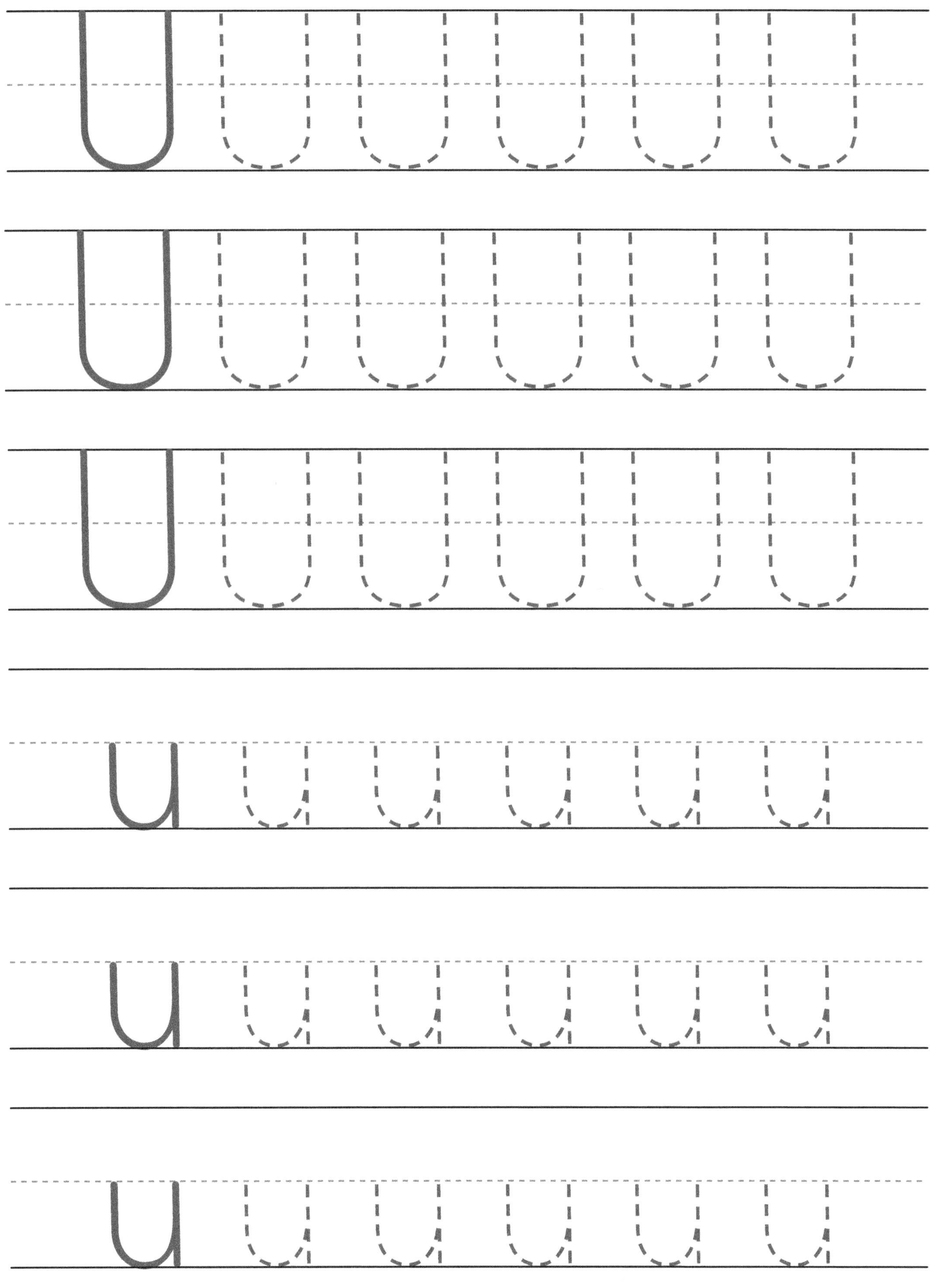

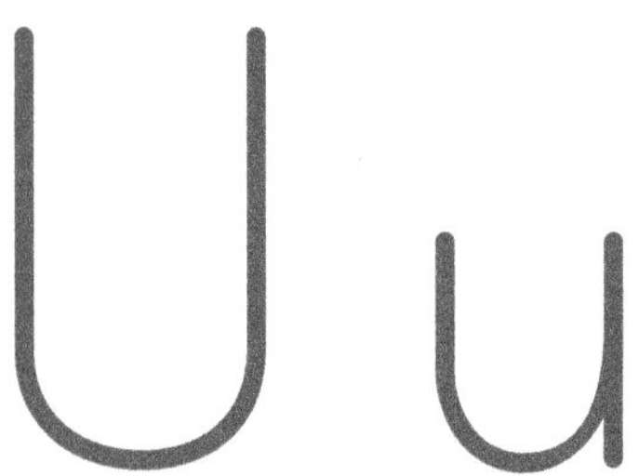

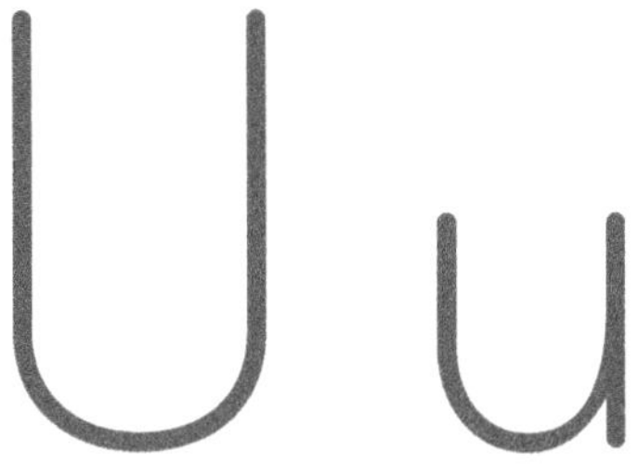

Connect

Upper case letter with its lower case

Do a circle on all letters of T
in upper case and lower case

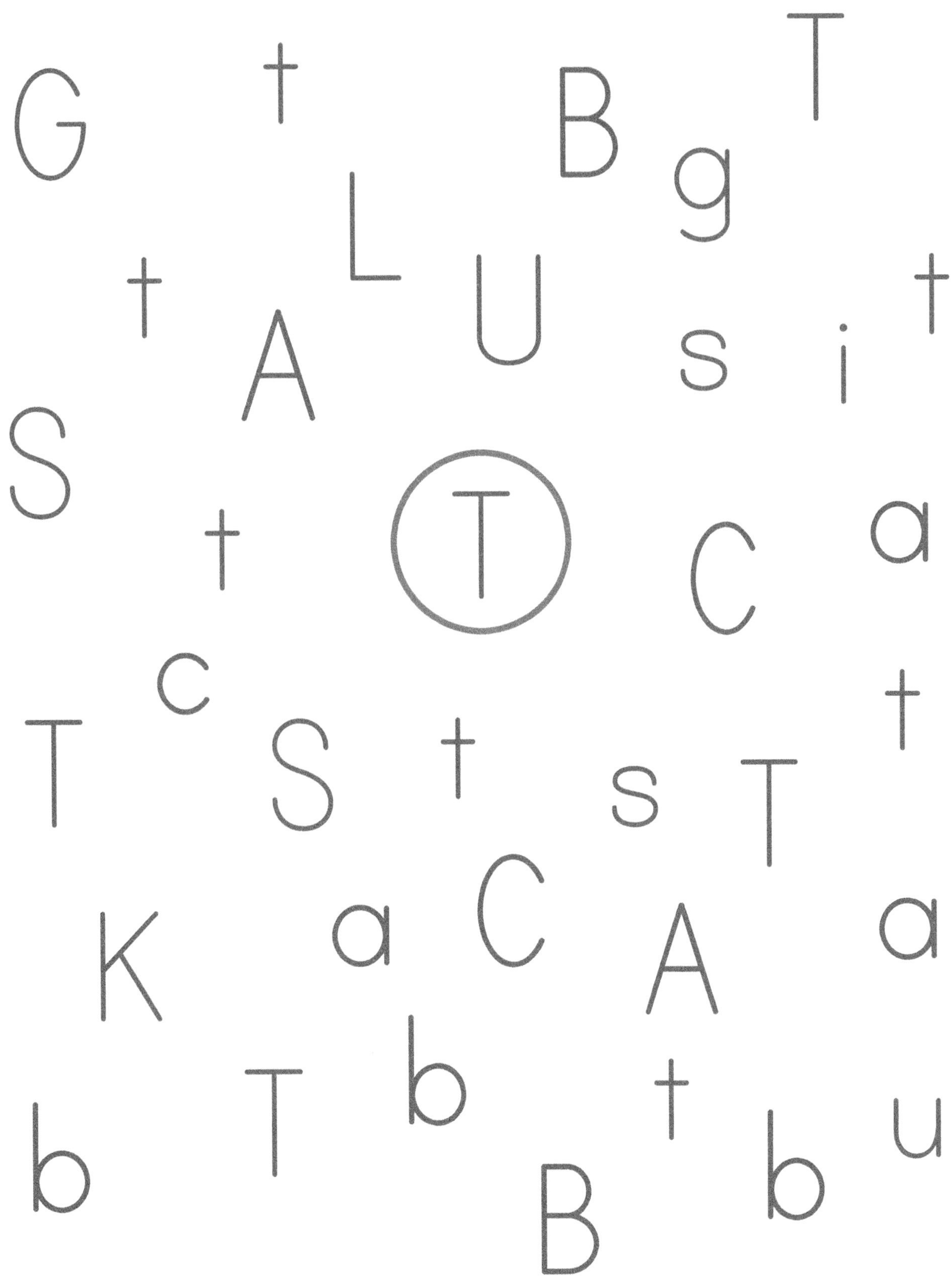

1 2
V
1 2
v
Van
V V V V V V
van
v v v v v v

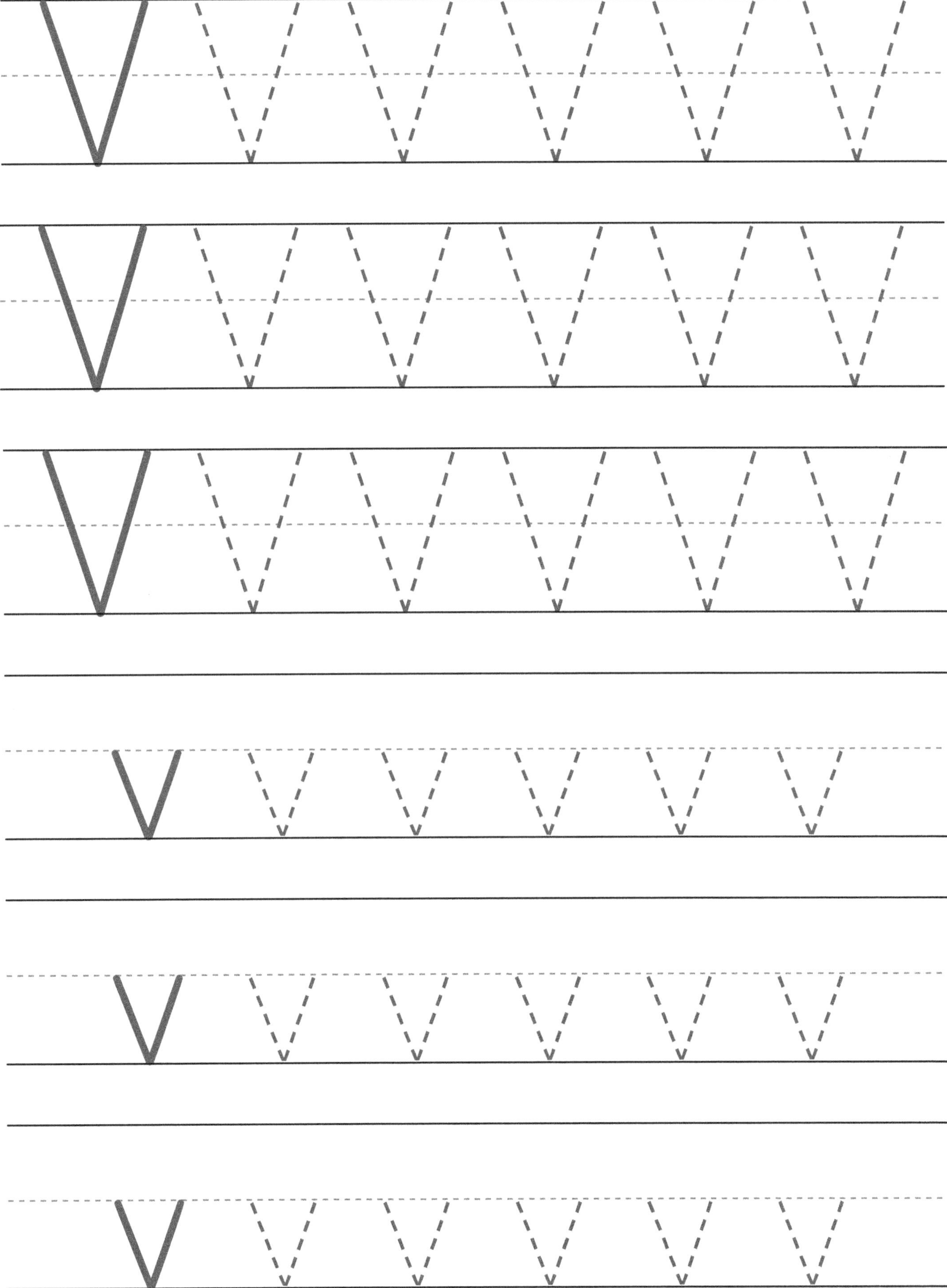

W w
Watermelon
W
watermelon
W

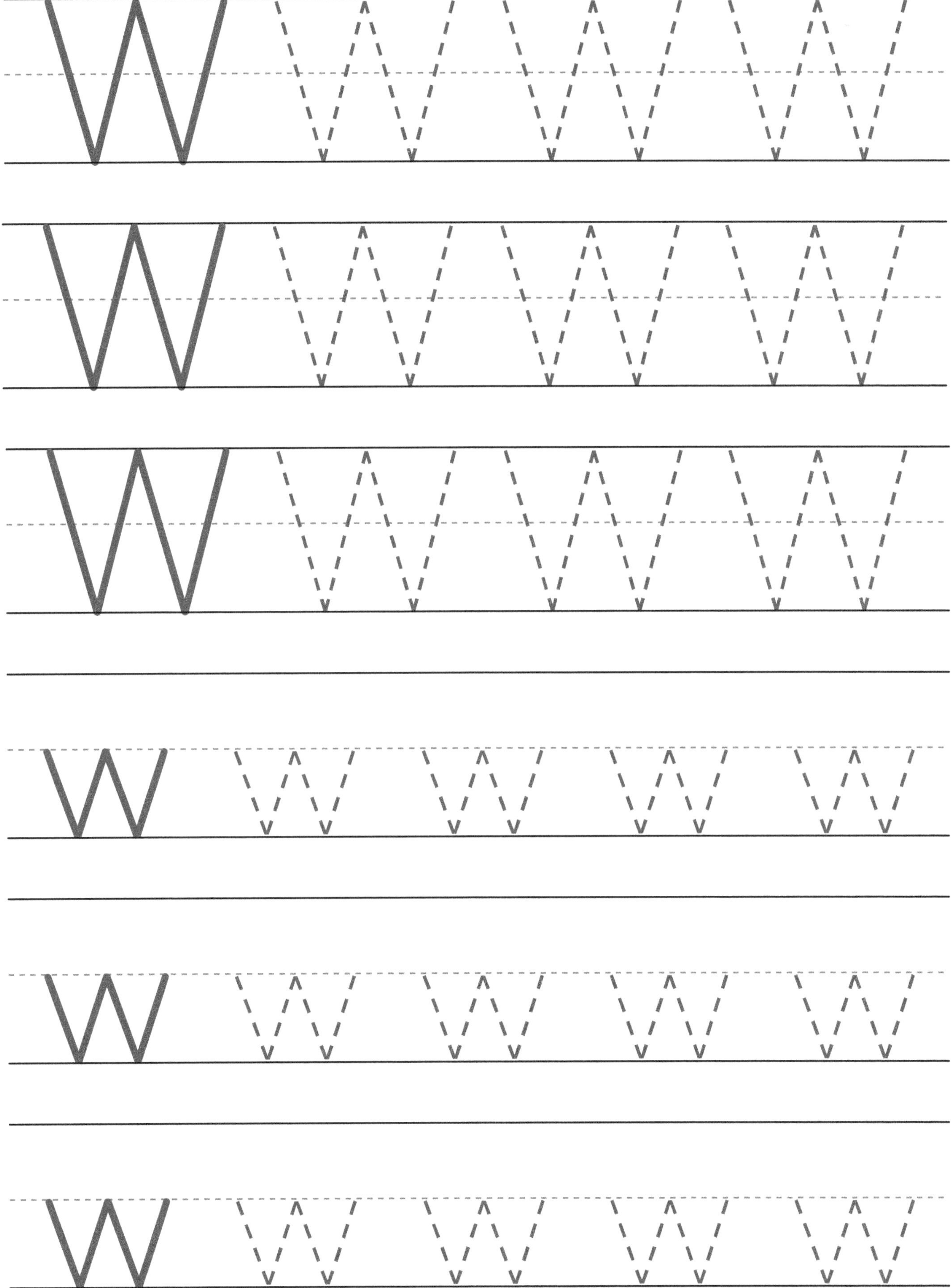

X-ray Fish
x-ray fish

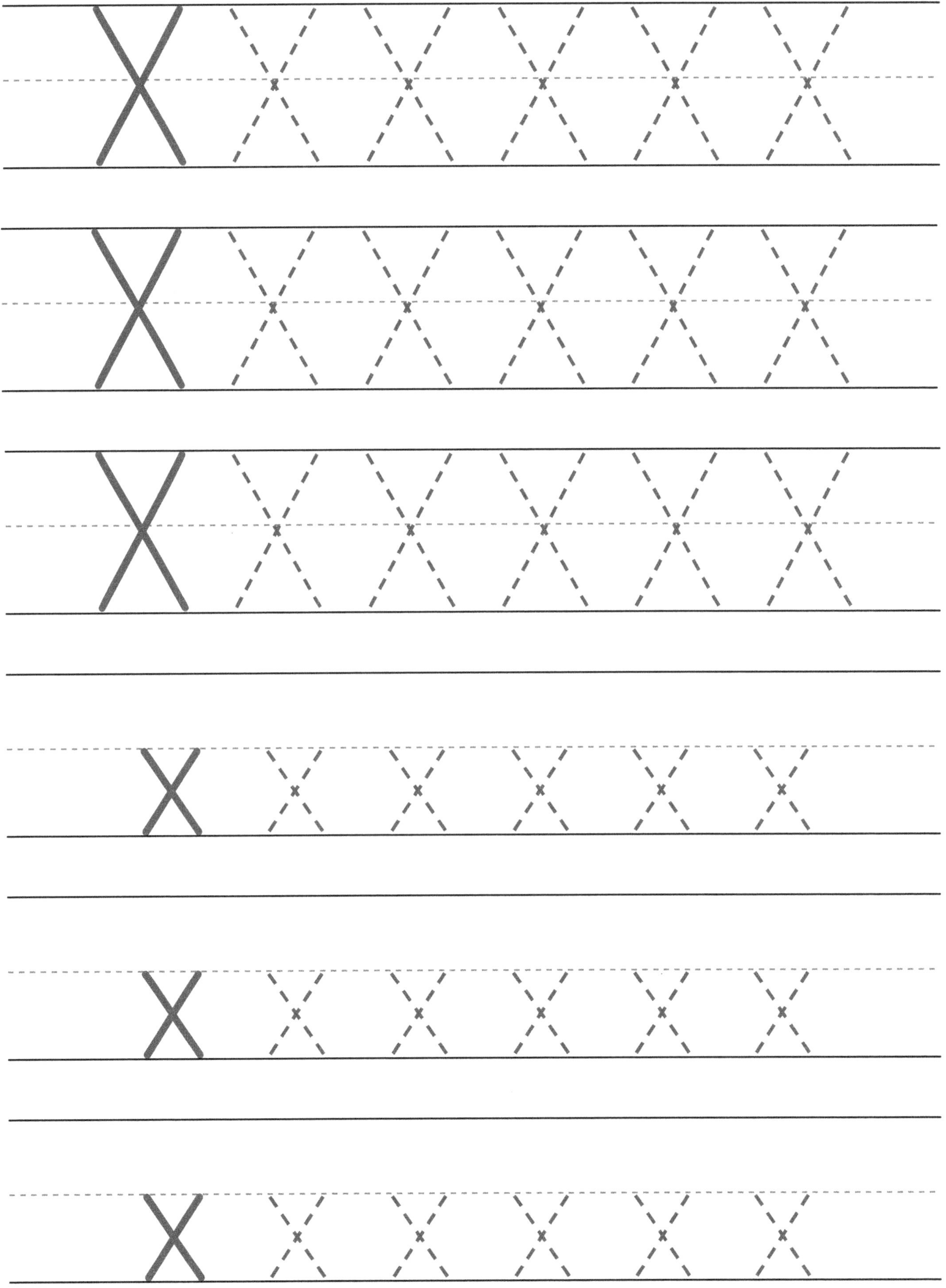

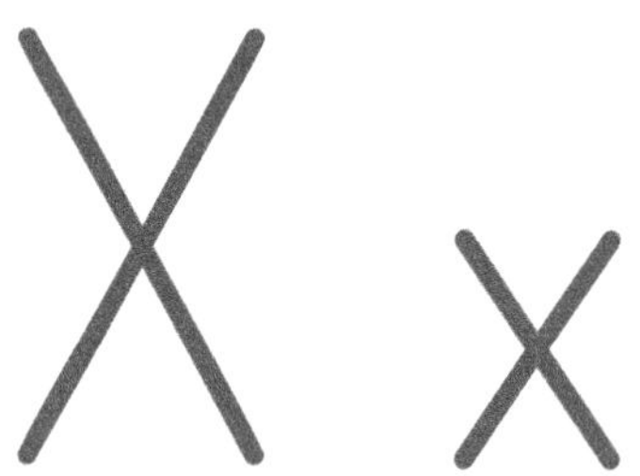

Connect
Upper case letter with its lower case

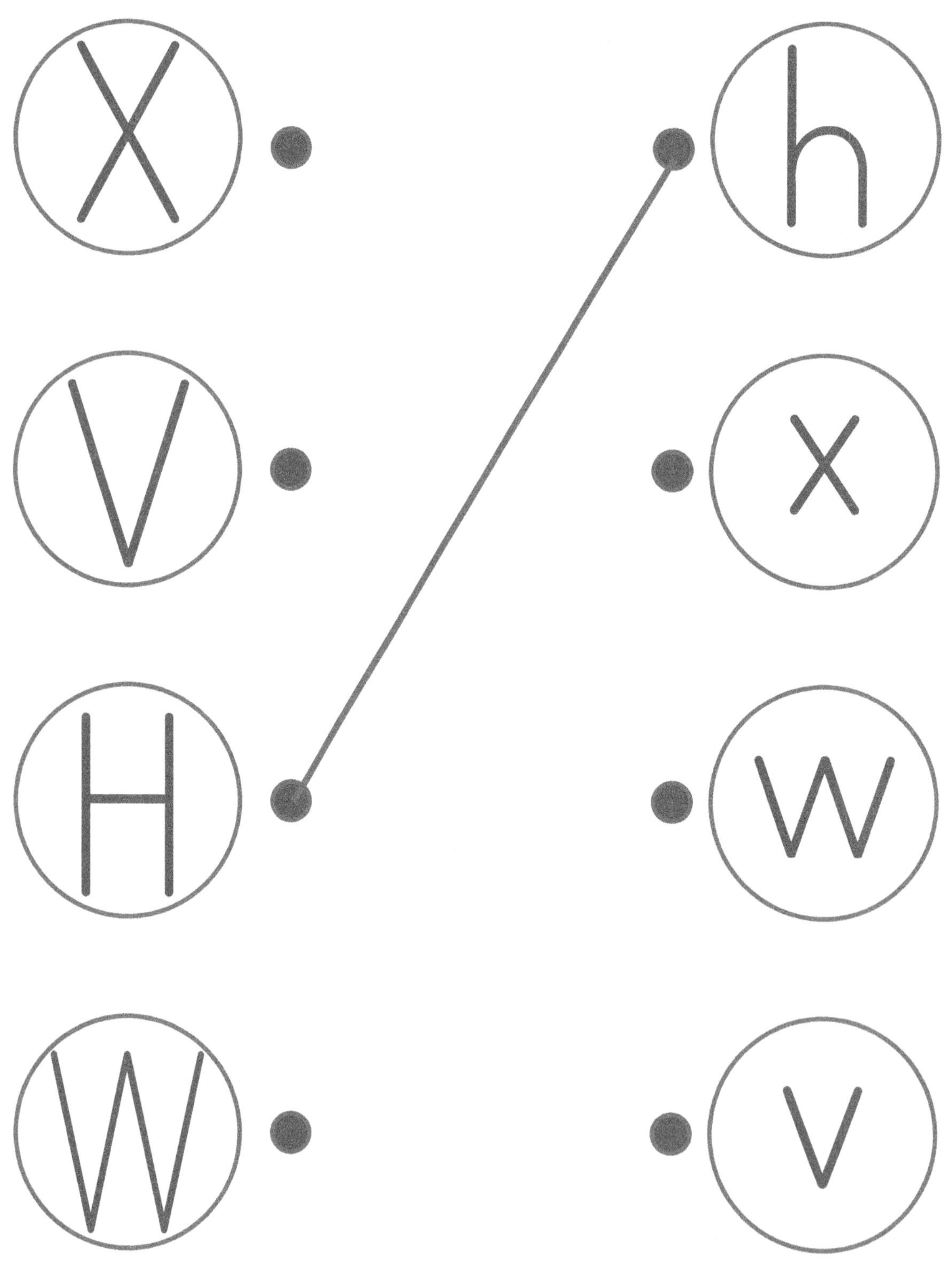

Do a circle on all letters of X
in upper case and lower case

1
2
3
Y
YOGUR
YOGUR
YOGUR
1
2
y
Yogurt
Y Y Y Y Y Y
yogurt
y y y y y y

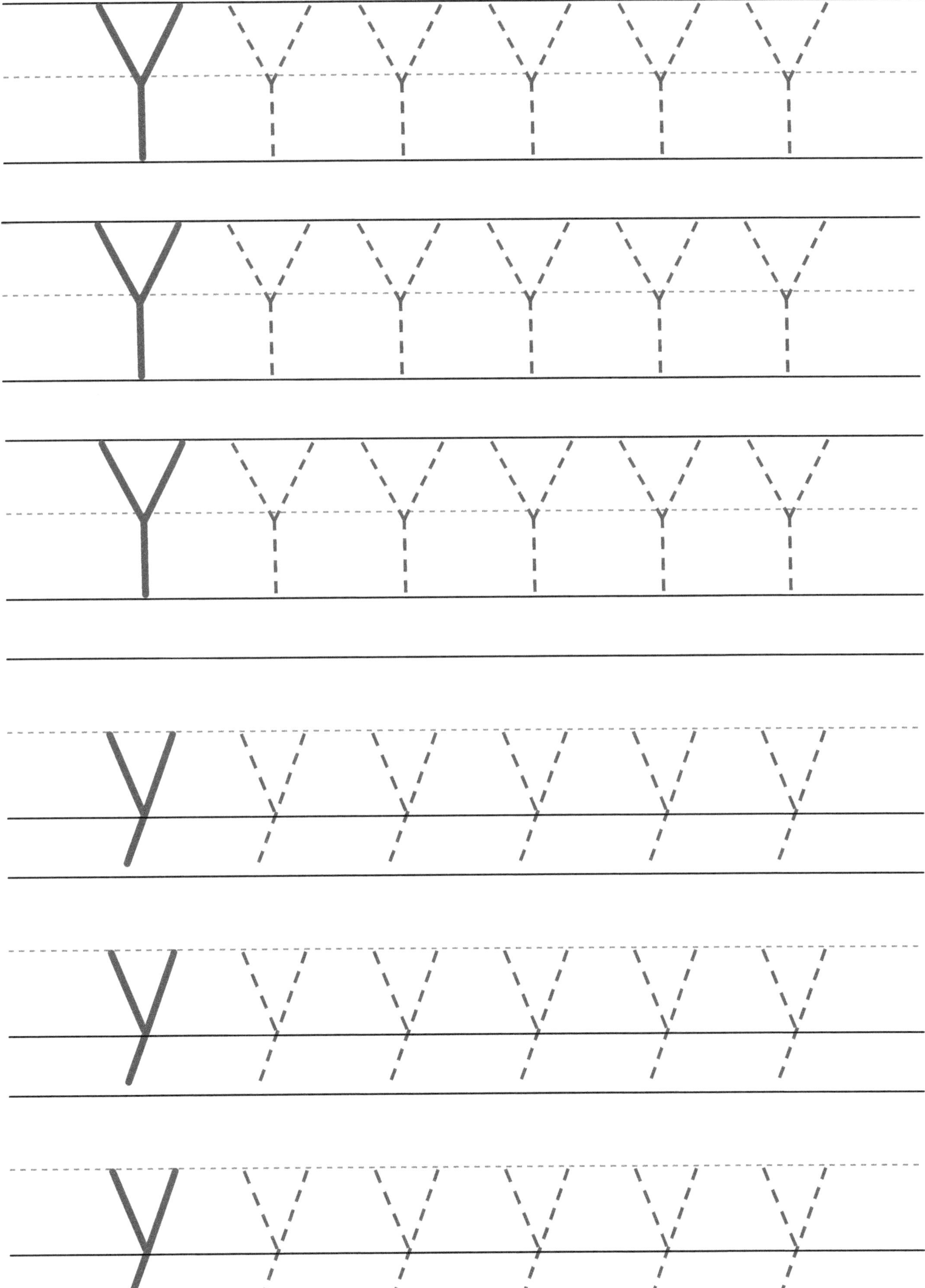

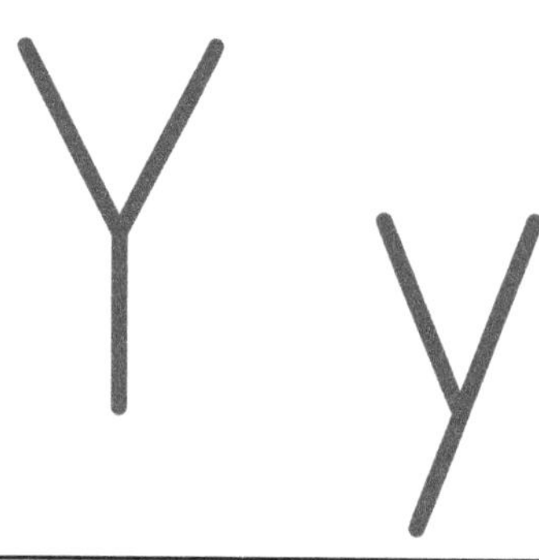

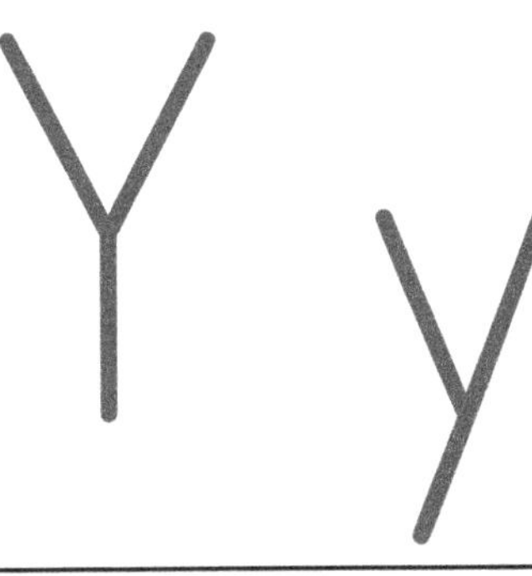

Zz

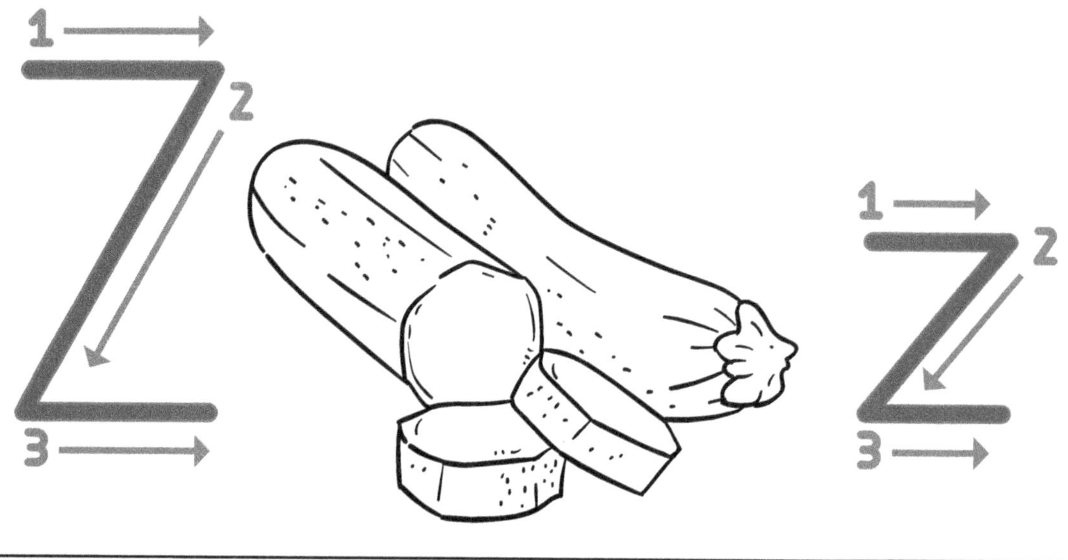

Zucchini

zucchini

Z Z Z Z Z Z

Z Z Z Z Z Z

Z Z Z Z Z Z

z z z z z z

z z z z z z

z z z z z z

Z z

Z z

Connect
Upper case letter with its lower case

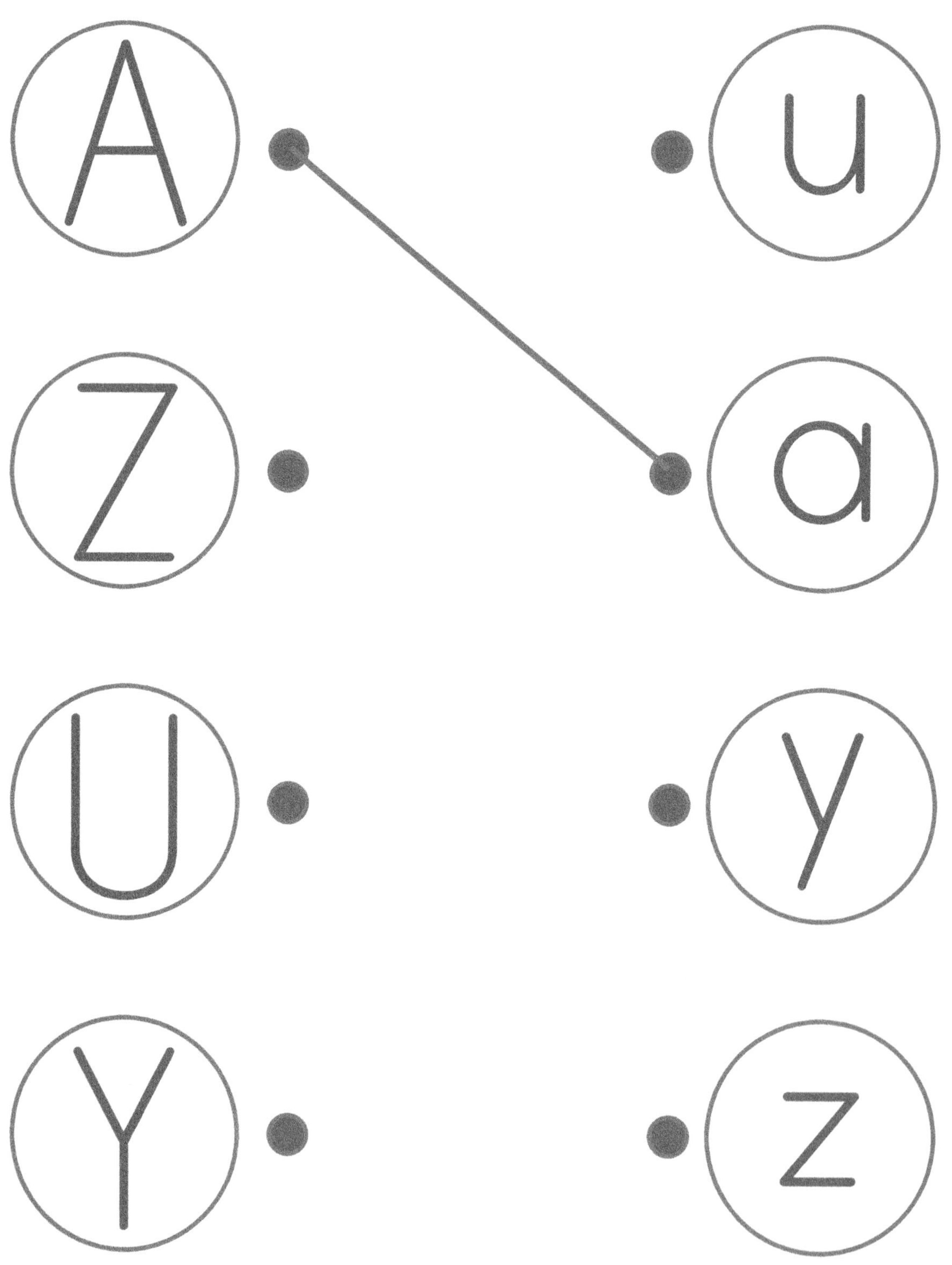

Do a circle on all letters of Y
in upper case and lower case

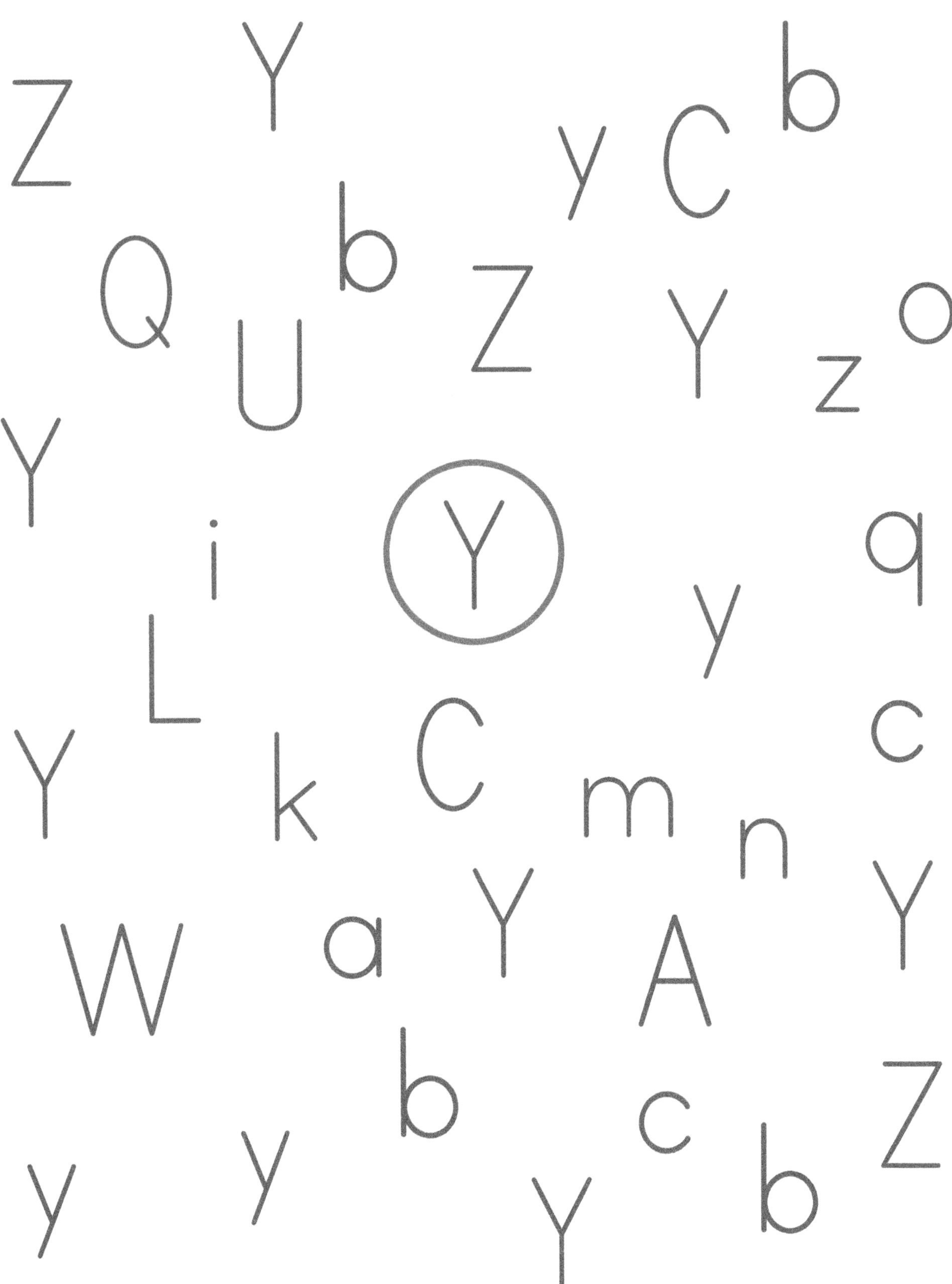

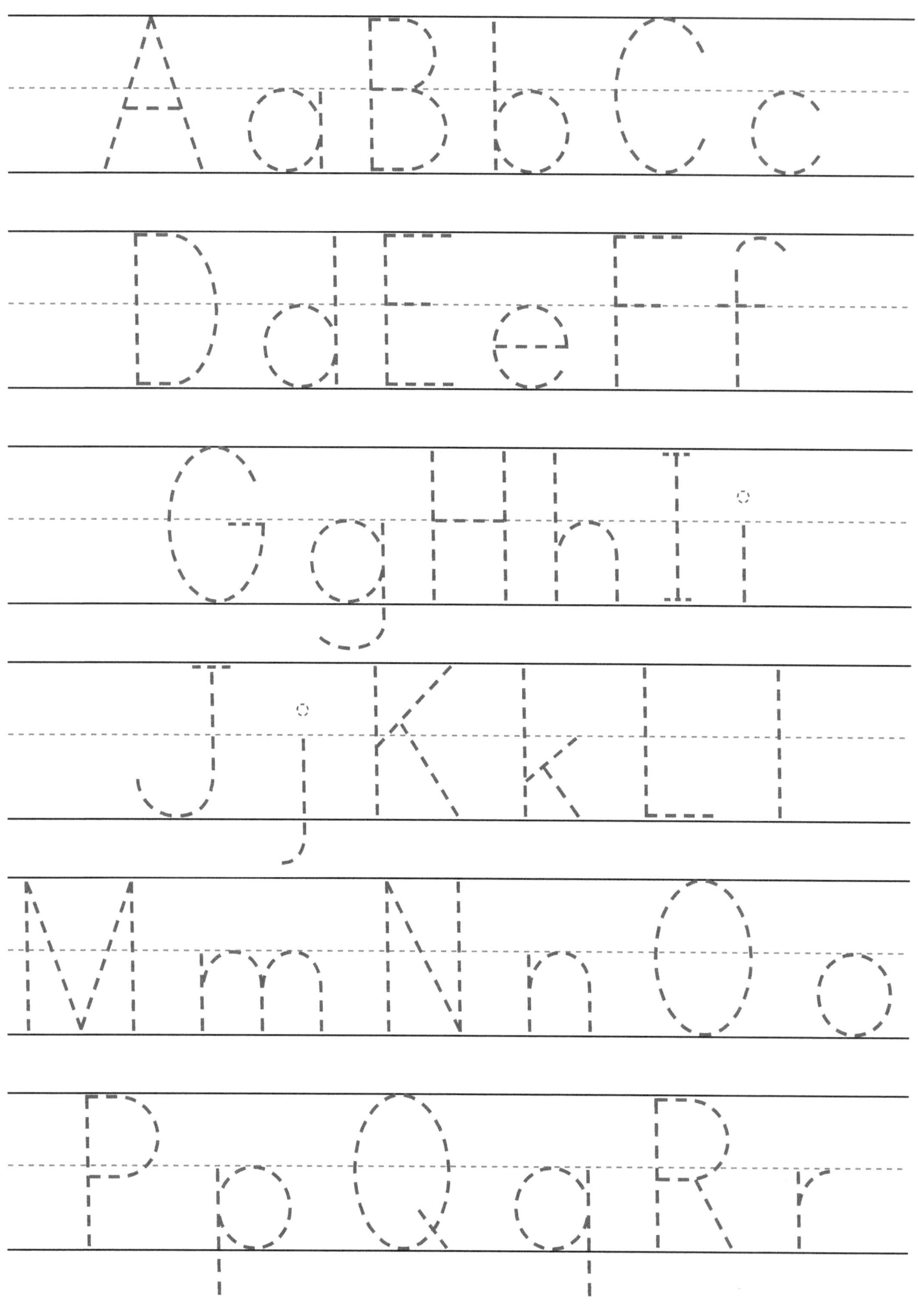

Aa Bb Cc
Dd Ee Ff
Gg Hh Ii
Jj Kk Ll
Mm Nn Oo
Pp Qq Rr

www.ingramcontent.com/pod-product-compliance
Lightning Source LLC
Chambersburg PA
CBHW081219130726
47997CB00009B/2722